Library of
Davidson College

The Tragedy of ERASMUS

The Tragedy of ERASMUS

A Psychohistoric Approach

Harry S. May

The University of Tennessee, Nashville

Piraeus Publishers

922.2
E65m

Copyright © 1975 by Piraeus Publishers, Saint Charles, Missouri. All rights reserved. No part of this work may be reproduced or transmitted in any form or by any means, electronic or mechanical, including photocopying and recording, or by any information storage or retrieval system, without permission in writing from the publisher.

Printed in the United States of America.

Library of Congress Catalog Card Number: 75-11159

ISBN: 0-913656-07-0

First Printing May 1975   76-8160

To Wanda

> I spit in the face of time
> that has transfigured me.
>
> Yeats

> Only now are we beginning to realize the obduracy of our own superstitions, our myths and the vast institutional structure in which they are embedded.
>
> George B. Leonard, in *Transformation, The Crack-Up of Civilization and the Rise of a New Society.*

CONTENTS

1. The Life of Erasmus 3
2. The Psychohistoric Approach 27
3. The Cup of Hate Runneth Over 36
4. The Betrayal of Reuchlin and Friends 55
5. Causes of Erasmus' Anti-Semitism 81
6. Crazy Quilt Theology and Ethics 95
7. The Reluctant Hebraist 109
8. The Probe 127
9. Humanism Reconsidered 157
   Suggested Readings 167
   Index 173

ACKNOWLEDGMENTS

When I started this work on Erasmus with trepidation and reluctance in the face of a traditional Historical Society, I was greatly encouraged by Professor Jacob Marcus of Hebrew Union College-Jewish-Institute of Religion in Cincinnati. Professor Lynn White, Jr. of the University of California also showed me the way toward improving style and psychological conclusions. At a time when financial grants were scarce The Memorial Fund for Jewish Culture in Geneva, Switzerland, came forth and generously supported my research and initial work on Erasmus. It was a heart-warming and uplifting gesture which this writer will always remember. Closer to home, The University of Tennessee at Nashville also responded to my repeated calls for help, financially and morally. A special word of thanks goes out to Miss Irene Glaus, Readers' Service-Librarian at UTN. Without her sleuthing and digging up all possibly available sources and monographs, dispersed throughout the land, the task of writing this work would have been overwhelming and costly. I also wish to acknowledge the cooperation I have received from my former employer, Vanderbilt University and its Joint University Libraries, Andover-Harvard Theological Library, the Central Library at Harvard, Yale University, The University of Tennessee at Knoxville, The Library of Congress, the University of California at Berkeley, the University of Georgia, the University of Kansas, the University of North Carolina, Drew University, Southern Illinois University and the Libraries of H.U.C.-J.I.R. in Cincinnati, Ohio. I wish to thank the Vanderbilt University Library for their help in securing the illustrations.

I have lived with Erasmus these past two years, but there was one more roommate: my colleague, Dr. Wayne Billings of our English Department at UTN. It was he who listened to my daily onesided dialogues with our anti-hero, Erasmus, and who gave me solace and good advice in my approach to this most difficult man of the 16th Century, Erasmus.

The Tragedy of ERASMUS

1
The Life of Erasmus

Even a brief review of Erasmus' life and reputation prompts some questions to disturb the esteem in which this man is still generally held. A review and the raising of such questions are the purpose of this chapter. But finding answers will call for an approach that needs some explanation, and so for now we may call to mind some of the facts of this wandering man's life as a humanist, writer, and controversialist.

He got off to a poor start with his birth, which became his secret affliction. He himself was in doubt about his proper birthplace, whether Gouda or Rotterdam, and about the year of his birth, whether 1466 or 1467. All he knew as a young boy was that his older brother Peter and he, christened Herasmus or Erasmus, were the illegitimate if not the incestuously conceived sons of a priest, perhaps named Rogerius Gerardus. This event alone made him hate his birthplace, his father and mother, neither of whom he ever mentions in his letters. He received his first education from Peter Winckler, the vice pastor of his church in Gouda, where young Erasmus must have been aware of, or must have been made to feel, his questionable background. Thus it is not surprising that we find Erasmus at the age of nine already on the move, away from Gouda on to Deventer, the monastic setting of the Brethern of the Common Life, an ascetic, mystically-oriented, but in its time a progressive order. There, Erasmus acquired a passion for writing letters, our source of deep inner revelations and confessions. He engaged in a dialogue with himself, in the absence of close friends or parents. Before he was sixteen his mother had died, followed soon after by his father. Thereafter, guardians appointed for the two brothers, sent his brother Peter to a monastery at Styn and took Erasmus to nearby s'Hertogenbosch where he was prepared for the severity of monastic life, which in those days meant the total subjection of mind and body, absolute discipline and deprivation. This was a poor start for a poor boy who suffered already from the stigma of his birth. But he also resented the "forced feeding" of scholastic knowledge and became later on in life a biting critic of the pedagogical method of his time. Next we find Erasmus in an Augustinian environment at St. Gregory's (near Gouda) where he became a friar and was ordained into the priesthood in 1492. Erasmus was introduced to the study of the Church Fathers and the Greek classics and the inner conflict between choosing a religious or secular career began to germinate.

For the next several years Erasmus sought security and a congenial post. In 1494 we find him working as Latin Secretary for Henry of Bergen, Bishop of Cambrai, where he met Battus, another school master. Henry, sensing his friend's dissatisfaction with a highly distracting and non-intellectual court life, obtained a small pension which enabled Erasmus to move to Paris to study theology. Typically, he was lodged in the poor house (*domus pauperum*) of the College of Montaigu. At an impressionable age Erasmus came under the influence of the daring reformer Jan Standonck, the spearhead of the Devotio Moderna which aimed at a housecleaning of the monasteries. Erasmus had found a soul-mate. Yet, despite his progress in learning, especially in Greek, he thoroughly disliked the atmosphere at Montaigu—he could not come to terms with the rigid discipline, the discomforts, and the abstinence. He rebelled, fell repeatedly ill, and in desperation ran back to Holland and then returned to Paris—but not to the College. He lodged in town, became a tutor and—as became typical of him in the years to come—began to scrounge for a living, looking always for patrons to support his leisure and his work. It was then that his friend Battus became the intermediary with the Lady of Veere, Anne of Borsselen, a relationship which ended in frustration and recriminations. But at last, Erasmus succeeded in persuading his friend and pupil Blount, the fourth Baron Mountjoy, to introduce him to John Colet and Thomas More in England where he went for a year. The two men had a good influence on Erasmus and encouraged him to study sacred literature and the classics. He even managed to save some money. However, on his way back to Paris customs officers confiscated his savings because foreigners were not permitted to take money out of England. Again he was faced with poverty.

The deep, unsettling tragedy of his life became apparent: Erasmus' life-style was to be that of an eternal wanderer and stipend-hunter; an intellectual vagabond to whom the world owed a living.[1] The beggar was born: in Paris he wrote dedications to Mountjoy, wrote devotional and moral compositions to Lady Anne and her son, coached pupils in Latin and Greek and gathered short sayings of classical authors, the *Collectanea Adagiorum.* Then came the plague and Erasmus fled to Orleans. Two years later he was back at the University of Louvain, near Paris, where it seems he was offered a teaching position which he declined. Pathologists believe he had a bout with syphilis, which had handicapped him. Perhaps he felt more comfortable without responsibilities, this young man of few needs. Or perhaps he preferred looking for outside support in the form of grants and scholarships.

His restless mind began to heed the admonition of his English friends: he wished to devote all his spare time to the study of the Fathers, the Epistles of St. Paul and Jerome in particular. Jobless, he could fulfill himself. He read Valla's *Annotations of the New Testament* and his own *Enchiridion Militis Christiani.* A master of Latin, he pleaded for the first time for the return of western man to the sources of early Christian life and strength, simplicity, and poverty. His theology was born out of his own simple, primitive living; his own life-style he patterned after his classical hero Plato. However, he did not wish to antagonize or embarrass the Church. Returning to the early sources of Christianity, Erasmus advocated a reduction of the Church's dogma and ceremonials; and in the new spirit of humanistic studies, he envisioned rather romantically a return of Christianity to the relevance of the ancient faith.

If we stop right here, some interesting questions come to

mind. Was Erasmus shocked by the growing urbanization of Christianity? Did he resent the already visible advance of commerce and industrialization of the society which might disrupt or discourage piety? Or was his stand a reflection of his own mental situation? Did he day-dream that a Christian Renaissance was really possible? Where did he fit in, this homeless, rootless Christian rebel who vacillated between Faith and Reason, Christian duty and resignation to the will of God? We can see already that at the age of forty Erasmus had not found a settled base of activity. Although he advocated reform, he did not do so from any particular place or as a member of any established circle of friends and associates.

Erasmus' journeyings and writings continued for the next three years. Lord Mountjoy invited him back to England in the fall of 1505 where he met the Archbishop of Canterbury, William Warham, Richard Foxe, Bishop of Winchester, and Baptista Boerio, the King's physician to the Court of Henry VIII. Baptista asked Erasmus to escort his two sons to Italy, the spiritual capital of all good Catholics and of Renaissance men. A year later he was in Rome, took his Doctor of Divinity degree at Turin, and managed his two young charges in Bologna. From there he began to negotiate with Aldus Manutius for the publication of his *Adagia* at Venice. By 1508 his three thousand adages or moralizing proverbs were completed, giving the work the new and final title *Chiliades Adagiorum*. Then he befriended Alexander Stuart, the legitimate son of James IV of Scotland and travelled with him to Siena, Rome, and the Campania. When Stuart returned to England, Erasmus was alone again, without patronage or reliable sources of income. Mountjoy came to his rescue and invited him back to England. Should he go to gratify his rich sponsor, or should he remain in Italy, in the circle of new friends: Bombasius, Musurus, Egantius, Lascaris, and Carteromachus, the men around Aldus, his publisher. If he went back to England, he would be closer to his sources of support, Colet, More, and Mountjoy. He decided to go and became the guest of Thomas More, whom he resembled physically, for three years. In the home of More's generous family, Erasmus wrote *In Praise of Folly (Moriae Encomium)*, a satire directed at all social classes enslaved by their

The Family of Sir Thomas More. From a sketch by Holbein, the Younger.

own follies, in which he recommended returning to the simple Christian life of yesteryear. Was this the work of a man who regarded himself an enlightened Humanist? Or was this an expression of Erasmian ambivalence? Was he at heart an anti-intellectual, as we would call him today? Or was he filled with hostility? And if so, against whom? Himself, society, the Church? We can already fathom the complexity of Erasmus' character.

While in England, he gave a few lectures at Cambridge on Greek and Jerome's epistles, and an English humanist by the name of Warham gave him a generous benefice, perhaps just to get rid of him. Another big-hearted soul, who appreciated the chronic financial embarrassment of our humanist, Aldington of Kent, allowed Erasmus a stipend for life in the form of twenty pounds per annum. He left England again in 1514 to supervise the printing of his works with Froben in Basel, Switzerland, and while there he was summoned to return to his former monastic life. After many entreaties with Pope Leo X in which he claimed clerical unworthiness, alluding to his possible incestuous origin which might defile the Church, he obtained his cherished freedom: he was allowed to live in the pagan world of Humanism.

Erasmus had brought to Switzerland with him an edition on Seneca and the Greek edition of the New Testament, which he had dedicated to Pope Leo X in gratitude for his clerical dispensation. After short trips to England and Germany, he settled in Basel, again surrounded by a coterie of young men, such as the three sons of John Amerbach, the publisher Froben's late business partner; also Beatus Rhenanus, J. Oecolompadius, W. Nesen, L. Ber, H. Glareanus and other humanists. From his publisher's center, Basel, Erasmus travelled for the next few years in the Netherlands, and accepted the appointment of Councillor of the young King Charles. Not to be outdone by a fellow Humanist, he travelled to Louvain again and joined Professor Hieronymous Busleiden in the founding of the Collegium Trilingue, a Liberal Arts School in which Greek, Latin, and Hebrew were to be taught, although the semitic tongue was never favored by Erasmus.

By that time, Erasmus had to face up to the Revolution of the Age: The Reformation. He himself did not mind at first Luther's attempt to reform the Mother Church from within. However, when Luther became volatile and aggressive, he disturbed the almost "feminine sensitivity" of the humanist who felt ruffled and unbalanced. Worse than that: Martin Luther tried to win him over to his side, which meant asking for a commitment. Erasmus shied away. He was at the height of his fame all over Europe—at least among those who had read his works but who had not met him in person. Erasmus was one of the most educated personalities of the time, while Luther addressed himself to the poor and ignorant. Presents and legacies began to pour in and Erasmus now lived at last in comfort. A final honor came to him when he was tendered the deanship of Deventer with the sum of 600 ducats and the promise for more if he would only declare himself against the Reformation. He declined, refusing to take sides. In his famous Cambridge letters he reflected upon his prestige, addressing

View of Nuremberg

himself to his friend Servetus, the Spanish radical anti-Trinitarian, he summed it all up:

In England there is not a bishop who is not pleased to receive my greeting, or who would not welcome me as a guest, or as a member of his household. The King himself shortly before his father's death, when I was in Italy, wrote to me a most loving letter with his own hand; he often speaks of me now with as much respect and affection as any one could possibly do, and whenever I wait upon him, he receives me with the greatest kindness, and regards me with such loving looks, that you may easily see that his sentiments are no less favourable than his words. The Queen has tried to get me to be her preceptor; and everybody knows that, if I cared to live even a few months at Court, I might heap up as many benefices as I liked. But I allow nothing to interfere with my leisure and studious labours. (7/8/1514)

Yet over the years he had developed ideosyncrasies: he could not bear the smell of English ale, the German stoves, the white wines of the Rhine and Mosel, the odor of fish or rough linen at hostels. Again, to preserve his freedom, or because he suspected competition from former Jewish, now Christian scholars (Marranos), he turned down a call to the Spanish University at Alcala, and avoided commitments to either orthodoxy or reform. However, he and Luther became entangled in the theological Reformation controversy of the time. Erasmus emphasized an aristocratic kind of Christianity, based on intellectual excellence. Here we see the influence of Plato. Luther's concern were the common people. And "man's individual free will was tempered by the power of God and by faith freely received."[2] In 1529 Froben died, and the triumph of the Reformation in Basel made Erasmus, the Catholic, an exile: he left for Freiburg in the Breisgau where he bought a home for six years. By 1535 he was back in Basel where he died in July of 1536, a tired and sick man. No priest or confessor was with him in his last hour.

Thus ended the life of this humanist who tried to live in two worlds: the classics and the world of Christian Humanism. He was a compulsive achiever and writer but looked upon by many as a petty-minded man, cantankerous, grovelling, and unable to hold friends, jealous of competitors (Reuchlin) indecisive in the face of grave issues (the Reformation) and ambivalent about his own feelings.

Perhaps one ought to be generous and attribute his character's strengths and weaknesses to the confusion brought on by the Reformation-Humanist era. Erasmus tried desperately to be both, a full-blooded orthodox Christian and an all-out Humanist-Renaissance man. The weakness of his Humanist scholasticism was a pedantic sense of erudition, a philological hair-splitting — at the expense of true intellectual development. Humanism rediscovered the past, but did not lead into the future. The very Latin style of Erasmus is a one-upmanship over Cicero, the antique master. The eulogistic gyrations and literary dedications of Erasmus have a touch of the insincere and panegyric—they have been compared to the sale of indulgences by the Church. By the same token Erasmus' contempt for the uncouth vernacular and his overemphasis on stilted word-form may have had another source: perhaps it was the expression of a man who abhorred defilement of any kind — a style which may have had some subconscious value for the writer.

Richard H. Popkin summarized Erasmian thinking quite accurately when he said:

Erasmus's ridicule of Scholasticism, although hardly a philosophical refutation of either its methods or its doctrines, created the generally accepted view that the medieval approach to philosophical questions was trivial and useless; ... Through his satire, his critical scholarship, and his undogmatic spirit Erasmus popularized a critical and questioning attitude toward accepted mores, institutions, opinions, undermining confidence in almost every area of traditional achievement.[3]

On the other hand his Christian Humanism expressed itself at times in a charming, affable and polished manner. And no one can dispute his classical or patristic learning. He was a prolific writer who dared to address himself to the often picayune quibbles of the times. And since some Humanists overdid their admiration of the classical writers such as Cicero, he stooped to name calling "pagans and obscurantists." This was when his biting irony came into play, and his mockery of human foibles. He believed in the undogmatic and ethical piety based on true love. Yet, with all of this: he, the humanist, and Luther, the Reformer, both were the dogmatists par excellence; brooking neither uncomformity nor deviation from the Faith, whether this was secular or religious.

Both traits came to haunt these two men. As for Erasmus, his psychological ambivalence made him a "heretic to both sides."[4]

Thus Erasmus' lifelong search for worldly security and intellectual happiness did not leave him with a greater sympathy for others who were poor in goods or in spirit. Instead his career made him famous, fastidious in literary style and personal habits, and restive in personal relationships. At this point we have to introduce another dimension of Erasmus' complex personality, his hatred of the Jews. The nature of his typically Germanic anti-Jewishness will cover a major portion of this book. However, we must make some references at this point: Erasmus was the victim of the medieval teachings of the Church regarding the Jews who lived at the periphery of Christian society. What disturbed Erasmus initially was their very presence, and that their Bible was held in good repute, especially amongst the Humanists. However, as his Christ-consciousness grew, so grew his anti-Jewishness in proportion. Both became his obsession and both made overwhelming demands on his life and his psychological well-being. What this fixation did to him is the major thrust of this investigation. At this point we can only say this: the Jews unhinged him. And no other humanist of his time was as plagued and persecuted by their presence as Erasmus was. They were his undoing, as we shall see, and this makes his Humanism so precarious and anti-intellectual.

Erasmus' career has won him many admirers. University libraries have been crowded for almost four centuries with Erasmian literature. Until very recently the vast majority of writers have sung the praises of Erasmus who was to most of them a man of letters, erudite in all aspects of Humanist thinking, whether in theology, linguistics, education, or the understanding of human follies. One will find hardly half a dozen or so monographs about the life of Erasmus which are critical of him, unless one consults books about the life of Luther, which naturally try to demolish Erasmus.

At best we find here and there an adjective that an author employed[5] to show his own displeasure with some of the manifestations of unkindness that somehow slipped through the mouth of his hero. But excuses were readily found. It was acknowledged that Erasmus was a brilliant mind housed in a sickly

Wreck of the Church. Johann Lichtenberger, 1497.

frail body, basically a man of peace, full of love, yet showing occasional outbursts of ill-temper which are only human.

Yet, the ever recurring theme about Erasmus was and still is that he was *Der Humanisten-Fuerst*, the Prince of Humanism.[6] One Protestant writer even suggested in 1937 that if his own church had the power to confer sainthood upon a person, Erasmus would be such a man indeed: "In conclusion, I have an audacious idea to express. Since Sir Thomas More, both wit and saint, has been duly canonized, may there yet be a chance for the dearest of his friends? ... Yet it would be audacious even to hope, though for me the hope is very tempting, that one day possibly *malgre lui*, he may be declared St. Desiderius Erasmus...."[7]

Rereading his lecture, Professor Rand, who admitted "that all he can do this evening is to make this hasty lecture," was quite inconsistent with some of his earlier criticism of Erasmus, whom he had called a parasite "who thought the world owed him a living, caddish, ungrateful to the greats of Cambridge who kept him from starvation," and self-serving in his cackling "protests from a safe corner of the barnyard" in his controversies with Martin Luther and John Reuchlin. But Rand concludes: "I should like to devote the remainder of my days on earth to reading every one of those eleven volumes from cover to cover, not with the idea of pouring another basket into the flood of books about Erasmus, but of having a good time."

Indeed, modern historians find much pleasure in reading Erasmus. He was a veritable Latin word-smith. Besides, he took on almost everybody of the establishment, from peasant to Pope, from heretic to Jew. So there is fun for all. And, depending on one's own make-up, we may smile occasionally at his witticisms. However, there is a sense of tragedy in his sarcasm, for it is trained always against somebody. He never laughs at himself. He never pokes fun at his own weaknesses. The Germans have a word for it, *Schadenfreude*, literally a joy derived from other people's suffering, sort of a sadistic pleasure to see others in pain. This is in essence the nature or Gestalt of Erasmian humor. It does not pain him to hurt or destroy others: it creates in him psychic satisfaction; like all sarcasm it gives vent to prejudice and hatred. It is one side of man's true, inner mirror.

In the concluding chapter on *Die Staatstheorie des Erasmus von Rotterdam*, E. von Koerber suggested that Erasmus knew what ailed him and what the mystery of his genius really was. Said he:

> Erasmus partially solved the problem for us when he declared that while he was at work a certain demon seemed to take possession of him and to carry him on without his will. His pen seemed to have a volition of its own ... Just as his powerful will compelled his frail and suffering body to do the bidding of his unconquerable spirit, so the literary impulse carried him on to utterances far beyond the capacity of his personality to realize in action. If Erasmus could have lived up to himself, he would have been the greatest of men.[8]

However, what is perplexing is that even twentieth century Jewish intellectuals, sensitized by Nazism, such as Margolin, Kisch, Zweig, and R. Friedenthal have fallen into this same trap. For reasons of their own they have believed that Erasmus heralded the coming of a new era. With him the Middle Ages, dark and sinister, had come to an end. The dawn of modern man, enlightened and generous, had arrived. The curtain had come down for good upon intolerance, bigotry, and superstition. Even the advent of the Hitler period did not detract these thinkers from their own preconceived notions. Perhaps the most tragic figure of this group is Stefan Zweig, who called Erasmus "the most brilliant man of his century." Granted, his small book on Erasmus was tendentious.[9] It was an intellectual's sensitive and deliberate approach appealing to good Germans to reject Nazism. Erasmus was saintly, Hitler was the opposite. Erasmus fitted into Zweig's scheme of things: he was a middle-of-the-roader, a pacifist, a Humanist and, best of all: he was a tolerant Christian in a world of political and religious turmoil. "There is nothing imperialistic about Humanism. ..." Zweig continued, "Every form of intolerance—and intolerance invariably implies misunderstanding—was alien to the doctrine of universal understanding; ... he was the first man of letters to advocate pacifist ideals." Unfortunately, Zweig misread his hero completely. Now, forty years later, one wonders whether this German-Jewish writer had ever read Erasmus' letters. So there is basically hardly any difference between a non-Jewish and a Jewish writer in their esteem for Erasmus, the Man for All Seasons, the *homo universalis*.

Erasmus. From a woodcut by Holbein, the Younger.

It has occurred to this writer that Erasmians in this century have studiously avoided an appraisal of their patron's anti-Semitism. They do not even make an attempt to distinguish between his enmity toward Judaism as such and his feelings about the Jewish People. From such investigation could have emerged perhaps a different picture from what we have of this humanist. Yet, our study is somewhat simplified by Erasmus' own words. He himself did not distinguish between the Jews and their religion. To him Jews were "criminals" and subversives as he states in his *Ratio*. [10] He used this nomenclature in the same way Soviet authorities do it in our time as they try Jewish dissenters against the regime in their courts of law. The whole gamut of criminality was invoked: economic, political, cultural, and racial. And when Erasmus referred to Judaism, then it was synonymous with Phariseism and Rabbinism. The alleged rejection of all Pharisees by Jesus, His critical attitude toward them as teachers and preservers of the Law (which he as an unsophisticated Galilean could not understand, or at least regarded as unsound and impractical), all of this rejection was adopted by Erasmus. He identified with his Christ, and the recorded words of the Gospel became Erasmus' Law. They were part and parcel of his Dogma which the Humanist uncritically accepted and transferred into hatred against Jesus' own people. It was Jesus' rejection of Jewish dogmatism (if it can be called that properly), which Erasmus accepted but then extended against an entire people who were also, according to the traditional medieval view, responsible for His death.

A lone voice to appreciate Erasmus' hostility toward the Jews was Gerhard B. Winckler, translator and annotator, who commented in his introduction to Erasmus' *Ausgewaehlte Schriften*, [11] "It is very difficult for us today to understand the theological antisemitism which Erasmus voices with great determination (*Bestimmtheit*), i.e. with exegetical arguments which because of their lack of objectivity therefore surprise, especially when he otherwise displays circumspection in the judgment of the texts of the Holy Scriptures. In his attitude toward the Jews of his time he does not represent, however, an isolated phenomenon, when one considers [by comparison] the harsh words of Luther against the Chosen People. Perhaps he found the theoretical basis for his attitude in Chrysostomus, whom he otherwise also held in very high esteem (*den er auch sonst sehr schaetzte*)." This short remark at the very end of a forty-page introduction indicates the embarrassment of Erasmus' translator in the year 1964. He wishes to clear Erasmus of his Christological blinders, but cannot quite succeed. He prefers to shift the blame to Johannes Chrysostomus, one of the guiding lights of Erasmus. But this should in no way serve as extenuating circumstances for the Humanist Erasmus. To bring in Luther, whose ill-tempered language seemingly outshouts that of Erasmus is pointless, for the difference in invective shows only a difference in temperament and style, not in degree of anti-semitism.

This writer offers the names of Johannes Reuchlin or Nicolas of Lyra as antithesis to Erasmian thinking. One thing becomes clear: Both men were far more "liberal" and tolerant: they were truly humane toward their fellowmen. Reuchlin had a host of friends and teachers studying Hebrew. Foremost among them was Pico della Mirandola in Italy (1490). Not only did he instruct him in the Hebrew language, but also introduced him into the mystical world of the Kabbala. In Austria at the Court of Frederick III at Linz he met the Emperor's physician, the Jew Jacob ben Yehiel Loens. And in Rome he continued his studies from 1498 to 1500 with Obadja Sforno of Cesena, the well-known commentator of the Pentateuch. This does not mean that Reuchlin was free from prejudice. Originally he regarded Jews as barbarians.[12] But his sense of justice forbade him to become violent.

Most interesting is Reuchlin's quote from the controversy with the renegade Pfefferkorn: "Every Christian may go to Law with them (the Jews), buy from them or make presents to them .... It is allowed to converse with them as St. Jerome and Nicolas of Lyra did." And lastly, "A Christian should love a Jew as his neighbor. All this is founded on the Law [of Moses]."[13] Erasmus would not even talk to a Jew. We learn that when he asked for a Hebrew instructor, he made sure that the man was at least a *bona fide* convert.

In the same category as Reuchlin belongs Nicolas of Lyra, whose great idol was the famous Hebrew commentator Rashi. The starting point for Nicolas was his dissatisfaction with the loose translations of the Bible. It is for this reason that he advocated, over one hundred years before Reuchlin, the study of Hebrew since it had a "special nature" of its own. Because of his constant reference to Rashi his detractors called him "Rashi's Ape." However, to remain in vogue, and as was expected, he did write

Frederich with Theologians. By Cranach, the Elder.

two anti-Jewish tracts in the "best scholastic tradition." In reality, they were defensive—to clarify Christianity for Christians and for Jews.[14]

The apologists for Erasmus will ask, but why then did he step forward in the defense of Reuchlin against charges of Judaising and the "freedom of Hebrew Studies"? Is not that proof enough that Erasmus was a Humanist? This writer's answer to the query is threefold. (1) Erasmus agreed in principle that for the sake of learning Reuchlin had the right to insist that Hebrew learning was necessary and desirable for the understanding of Old Testamental sources. However, he himself warned scholars not to overdo it lest they themselves become Jewish sympathizers and fellow-travellers (theologically speaking, of course). (2) His erstwhile defense of Reuchlin cooled off considerably when the pressure was on, *i.e.* when he himself became highly criticized and was almost called a "Jew-Lover" and as a consequence eventually betrayed Reuchlin. (3) Psychologically speaking, a possible answer for his behavior could be that subconsciously Erasmus felt that Reuchlin was right and he was wrong, that Reuchlin was the better scholar! Perhaps he even admired the "friend" for his forthrightness and cogent thinking. But then he caught himself: defending or loving Jews would have been tantamount to a betrayal of Christ. He could not love both. That was his obsession or sickness. To sharpen our case, we can make history even more relevant by saying: Hitler was also a sick man, though some Christians regard him now, theologically speaking, as the anti-Christ. To this writer Hitler was the twentieth-century "negative climax" of what Christianity had produced. In his twisted mind, he reversed early Christianity, by re-superimposing Roman Paganism (*panem et circenses*) over a missionary Christianity. But the Myth remained the same: The Jews were the enemies of mankind. And his dogma—although basically political—had strong religious and Christian overtones. His pagan missionaries and subvertors almost conquered the world, and his crooked cross fluttered over Europe, incidentally in the same territories where western Christianity had held sway for sixteen hundred years. Hitler was the exponent of a new dogma, a New Gospel, infallible and "man-saving," and heretics or dissenters were put to the stake (gas-chamber). Parenthetically, Erasmus and Luther both also recommended the "elimination of the Jews" in some of their many letters, although they might have been satisfied with their ejection from the western world to make it *juden-rein*, free of Jews. That would have been their sixteenth-century Final Solution. But then, Erasmus was too cowardly to advocate physical mass-violence.[15] Our pro-Erasmians explain here his paranoid behavior again by saying that he was a sick person to the point of hypochondria, as he was, no doubt. And a similar case could be made for Luther, who was known to have had gastric trouble, spells of depression and melancholia.[16]

But is illness really an excuse for man's hatred against his fellowman? Erasmus is so closely linked to the Reformation, approaching closely the bridge that spans precariously the old and new epochs in the history of western man, that he is vital for our understanding of the inner schism in western Christendom. He brought a new dimension into European scholarship (though still a scholastic himself in so many ways), namely the utilization of Greek and early Christian scholarship, to mediate between the dogmatists on the left and right, only eventually to fall himself into his own self-made trap. Erasmus' tragedy is that his humanistic approach to learning and teaching ended where he did not intend to mediate and reconcile: in the theological "No-Man's-Land" of intolerance, prejudice, and unyielding, dogmatic Catholic stiffness. If, as some scholars believe, there is something of an Erasmian theology, although unsystematic and lacking innovative and speculative luster, then these men will undoubtedly arrive at the conclusion that Desiderius Erasmus of Rotterdam was not a bridge-builder or conciliator within the feuding Christian family, but was one more dogmatist who was instrumental in the polarization of western Christendom.

He was in the last analysis a part-time Medievalist and a part-time Humanist. The main three theologies of the sixteenth century evolved around Luther, Erasmus, and the counter-reforming Papacy. And all three left their imprint on our society. Their legacy was not an enlightened faith, but one of bitter controversy and mutual persecution, culminating in long religious wars and to some extent affecting events all the way into the twentieth century. While Christians killed Christians in the process, the Jews were the main victims. Man only has to dare study the Jewish Middle Ages, which lasted much longer than the Christian Middle Ages. Luther and Erasmus, in sum, were unaware of the truth that the Reformation squabble was nothing else but a Teutonic version of the highly competitive Italian humanistic Renaissance.

In retrospect, we can therefore understand (though never condone) the antisemitism of first and second generation Humanists. We have to keep in mind also that western Christianity was watched from many viewpoints, by Jews and Moslems alike.[17] It is this inner conflict within the western Church which led eventually to its fragmentation that these Humanists wished to cover up through an offensive of their own against unorthodoxy and heresy. Defending his Faith, Erasmus became an offensive missionary, clothed in cap and gown, covering up his infirmities and frustrations with an irrational Jew-hatred that even further undermined his health until he died at about seventy, not at peace with himself or with a united Christian World for which he had fought his own Don Quixote battle. Or was this man who understood the battle cry of his humanist colleagues: *Ad fontes*, back to the sources of antiquity, nothing else but a religious Minnesinger in love with his Christ, a really "tragic figure" who did not know which time to choose: the old or the new?[18] Or was he somewhere along the line subconsciously "aware" of the imperfection of his own personal Christian Faith?

The study which follows will therefore make an attempt to unravel Erasmus' personality by means of a psycho-historic investigation. However, this writer wishes to caution the reader: he regards himself a historian first. His attempt to utilize modern psychological findings and phenomena, motivations and causations both, will serve only one purpose, and that is to show his disagreements with other historians. He will not engage in entering into the badly split psychological schools and sectarians that arrive at "very different conclusions about identical phenomena," as Professor Lynn White, Jr. observed.[19] To this writer it is of little consequence how psychologists or historians argue. The purpose of this book is to show Erasmus for what he really was, as human with all his virtues and failings. This writer does not feel alone in critiquing the Great Humanist. Rudolf Pfeiffer quoted R. Haym:

The Life of Erasmus 23

One hundred fifteen years ago Rudolf Haym wrote a critique of Erasmus in his *Prussian Yearbooks* (1859): "In Erasmus we find the embodiment of complete weakmindedness (Schwachmutigkeit), total vanity . . . the cowardly lack of character which afflicts to this day the self-satisfying scholarship and literary profession. . . . The core for his love for peace was self-love, and the reverse side of those talents through which he delighted his contemporaries, was a low disposition (*niedridge Gesinnung*) . . . . The Erasmian elegance was amoral." Erasmus is depicted by Haym—as Mommsen said about Cicero, the humanist's idol—as a characterless prattler.[20]

And again, Pfeiffer, in his *Humanitas Erasmiana,* tried to go to the root of the Erasmus' character and held that there "is at the very core of the German character a deeply rooted resistance against the principle of *Humanitas*" which can only be overcome by the inner will of the individual. The reader will not always agree with this author's findings. Hopefully this volume will give birth to a renewed discussion about Erasmus.

NOTES

[1] Preserved Smith in his *Erasmus* (New York, 1969) makes this observation: "Erasmus was by nature a nomad. Never did he live as long as eight years consecutively in the same place."

[2] G. L. Mosse, *The Reformation* (New York, 1970), pp. 18-21.

[3] *Encyclopedia of Philosophy*, Vol. III (New York, 1967).

[4] Lewis W. Spitz, *The Renaissance and Reformation Movements* (Chicago, 1971), p. 297.

[5] G. R. Elton in *Erasmus and the Age of the Reformation* (New York, 1963), p. 282, calls Erasmus "a fence-sitter." R. H. Bainton: *Erasmus of Christendom* (New York, 1969), pp. 285-299. J. C. Margolin, *Erasme par Lui-meme*, Douze annes de bibliographie Erasmienne, (Paris, 1965), pp. 186-188. W. P. Eckert, *Erasmus von Rotterdam* (Cologne, 1967), II, pp. 636-44. H. Lutz, *Umanesimo e Rinascenze in Germania* (in *Grande Antologia Filosofica*, Milan, 1964), XII, pp. 685-89.

[6] Guido Kisch, *Erasmus' Stellung zu Juden und Judentum* (Tuebingen, 1969).

[7] Edward Kennard Rand, *Horace and the Spirit of Comedy* (Houston, 1937), pp. 92-117.

[8] E. von Koeber, *Die Staatstheorie des Erasmus* (Berlin, 1967), p. 463.

[9] Stefan Zweig, *Erasmus of Rotterdam* (New York, 1966), p. 106 ff.

[10] Werner L. Gundersheimer in his study, *Erasmus, Humanism and the Christian Kabbala*, uses the term anti-Semitism for the first time in *Journal of the Warburg and Courtauld Institutes*, XXVI (Freiburg, 1963), pp. 38-52.

[11] Gerhard B. Winkler, *Erasmus Ausgewaehlte Schriften*, Wissenschaftliche Buchgesellschaft, Vol. III (Darmstadt, 1967), p. XXXVIII.

[12] Henrich Grätz, *History of the Jews* (Philadelphia, 1941), Vol. IV, pp. 422-463.

[13] Jewish Publication Society (Philadelphia, 1941). See also L. Geiger's article in the *Universal Jewish Encyclopedia*, Vol. 9 (New York, 1943), p. 145.

[14] H. Heilperin in *Rashi Anniversary*, Vol. 1, 1941, pp. 145-147.

[15] Luther had an ambiguous view on bloodshed, as his reaction toward the Peasant Revolt shows.

[16] Eric Erickson, *The Young Man Luther* (New York, 1958).

[17] In his book *Elizabeth I* (Chicago, 1974), p. 144, Paul Johnson wrote: "All the nations of Europe were close to the brink of civil conflicts which reflected the great international war of faith; the Continent was crusading against itself. In England, thanks to *her* father's quest for an heir (i.e. Elizabeth I), religious change had been imposed, or directed from above, and legalized by statute; there at least, civil war—so far—had been avoided. Elsewhere, Reform collided with established authority. Germany was to become a battlefield. Italy was already a theatre of violent persecution. In Spain, royal armies clashed bloodily with armed sectaries, Moors and Jews. In 1559 the religious revolution had struck Scotland with pent-up force. From 1560, and for the next thirty years, it convulsed France. In 1566, it came to the Low Countries."

[18] R. Friedenthal: *Luther, Sein Leben and seine Zeit* (Munich, 1967 and 1971), p. 130.
[19] This author's correspondence of August 3, 1972.
[20] Rudolf Haym, *Prussian Yearbooks* (Berlin, 1931), p. 21.

2
The Psychohistoric Approach

The history of man is not only the assessment of outer conflicts such as wars, murder, and revolutions, but also of man with his inner conflicts, steadily gnawing from within, driving him to decisions and unpredictable actions. After all, man is not a rock; he is flesh and blood and has a psyche which can be jubilant or it may be filled with suffering which nobody can escape. The psychohistorian recognizes man for what he is, filled with mixed emotions. It is therefore not enough for psychohistorians to become "see-ers" (Charcot) or to lay out the historical fabric of man's personality, to paraphrase A. P. Thornton, but to try to "disentangle truth from fiction." What is called myth in history then is man's attempt either to misread history or to dream up convenient distortions needed for his own self-esteem or need for security.[1] The tragedy of it all is this: it is nearly impossible to dislodge a myth, especially when it is hundreds of years old, as in the case of Erasmus.

Do psychohistorians have to be also experts in psychology in order to appraise and interpret history? Today's historians have to be at home in political science, economics, sociology, religion, and humanistic studies. That was not so twenty-five years ago. So, why shy away from psychology? Why cannot historians delve carefully into the dark abyss of man, his psyche, and reconstruct the past, "filling the inevitable gaps and selecting issues and concepts that seem relevant."[2]

When we write about Erasmus, it is implied that we are going to be selective; we will show his ambiguity toward his friends and enemies and ask: Why? We will put his Humanism under the magnifying glass and dissect it. We will do the same with his religious, political, and educational views. But lastly and most poignantly: we shall probe into his unconscious and analyze his attitude toward the Jew, his favorite whipping boy. This attempt to "explain" Erasmus' character-makeup will, in the end, shed new light upon his inner structure and thus open the way for a renewed reevaluation of his personality. We shall go one step further: we shall concentrate on Erasmus' antisemitism, his own psychological affliction. Erasmus' religious prejudices in all of their dark and sinister implications make it possible for us to really analyze him. A man may "cover up" his happiness or sadness with a stoic mask. But nobody can hide or suppress prejudices for long. They must eventually explode to the surface; otherwise they will affect a man's health, physical and mental. Prejudices degenerate into hatred, and — in the absence of an imaginary or a weak foe — will sooner or later convert to acts of persecution, whether physical or intellectual. Erasmus' type of antisemitism furnishes us with a magic key as it represents the lowliest yet most revealing aspect of a psyche's anatomy. Wolman was right when he observed:

It seems therefore that the interpretation of history must descend from its Olympus and join other natural sciences that analyze the behavior of individuals and groups. Freud has largely contributed to such an approach to history. He tore down the sacrosanct stories about the alleged human kindness and morality and exposed the true human nature from its animalistic roots to its most sublime cravings. Man is neither beast nor angel, but his nature is a strange, irrational, often incomprehensible mixture of both. Culture to Freud meant restrain, and "much of our most highly valued cultural heritage has been acquired at the cost of sexuality and by the restriction of sexual motive forces," stated Freud in his last and final summary of psychoanalysis.[3]

Erasmus in his own time made history. He was an involved man, involved with people and events. He was also at times involved with himself on the conscious level. After all, he had to survive the onslaughts of his time: the Reformation, the Peasant Revolts, the struggle within the Church and the spread of heresy

The Psychohistoric Approach

Erasmus of Rotterdam. By Holbein, the Younger.

which included also another type: Capitalism. His human behavior was governed by these events. Erasmus at times bent with the winds or resisted the currents of a new era. This makes him a participant in history, a very involved person. The crucial question is this: Was he also responsible for the course of events in his own time, or was he irresponsible? These are embarrassing questions because Humanism demands that man be a responsible actor on the stage of history, however small, or however short-lived. Erasmus was one of the first generation of northern Humanists. He was a man who lived at a time of great change. It was his passion to be the changer of men. As Wolman observed, "the laws of nature cannot change, but human behavior can."[4] Erasmus, as we will interpret him, was a man of flux — certainly not fixed in any of his intellectual positions. But what strikes historians today, four hundred years after his death, is that his "concept of identity" — as Eric Erikson calls it — was in actuality a process of a "flux upstream," that he tried to "buck" the men and institutions of his time, only to be shattered upon the rocks of his own making, with the wreck of his own humanistic efforts to renew the Church and medieval learning and to bring to man a western Christendom that was to be saturated with classical and modern learning.

Erasmus sought to protect himself inwardly as well as outwardly. However, he did not find psychic security in endorsing any established institution or existing group: these he often attacked. His behavior resembles that of a human type which has its own name — Protean Man. Let us take an example of his behavior.

We have noted that Erasmus' sarcasm invariably is aimed at someone, and aimed to hurt. When Robert J. Lifton speaks of Protean Man, he suggests a person who has "a profound sense of absurdity, which finds expression in a tone of mockery." Erasmus was such a person. What historians and literati have wrongly called his sense of humor or wit was nothing else but biting sarcasm against a rival, a friend, or an institution. It was born out of a deeply felt sense of guilt. And he suffered from it, often unaware of what was at the root of his suffering. Lifton speaks of the "hidden guilt" that was caused by a lack of outlets for his loyalties. Perhaps Erasmus had reasons for these guilt feelings, such as leaving his monastic enclosure. But even if he had no real feeling of guilt, evil doings, and sinfulness, we do know that he had a "nagging sense of unworthiness, anxiety and resentment."

These too have origin in symbolic impairments and are particularly tied in with suspicion of counterfeit nurturance. Often feeling himself uncared for, even abandoned, protean man responds with diffuse fear and anger. But he can neither find a good cause for the former nor a consistent target for the latter. He nonetheless cultivates his anger because he finds it more serviceable than anxiety, there are plenty of targets of one kind or another beckoning, and because even moving targets are better than none.[5]

Anticipating already some of our findings, it was Professor Lewis Spitz of Stanford University, who summarized his own feelings about the Humanist:

The story of Erasmus is so common that, to turn a phrase from Chaucer, every wit that hath discretion knows all or part of it. And yet Erasmus remains elusive, a proteus, a man of a hundred faces. Immortalized by Holbein, Quentin Metsys, and Duerer, he looks out from the canvas with an enigmatic half-smile, an expression suggesting the complications of his personality. Small wonder that straightforward Frederick of Saxony commented that this was an amazing little man, for one never knows where one stands with him. He was gifted with a quick and ready wit, with unusual charm and brilliance. For all his correspondence and superficial gregariousness, he was a lonely monarch who gave of himself without reservations to no one. He was no confessor, no fighter, no great man. He abhorred disturbances to the point of appearing to many contemporaries to be a timorous neuter. He was a valetudinarian, loving good living and creature comforts, petulant, querulous, flattering, deceptive, and vindictive. He saw his own weakness and feared that in case of a conflict he would like Peter deny his friends. He could speak almost disinterestedly of the tragic deaths of his friends Fisher and More. "Not all have sufficient strength for martyrdom," he confided.

But we may suspect that he lacked "strength for martyrdom" because he lacked loyalties. A lifetime's wandering from one opportunity to another left him still insecure in human ties, despite his eventual fame and material comforts.

NOTES

[1] Robert Waelder, "Psychoanalysis and History: Application of Psychoanalysis to Historiography," in B. B. Wolman's *The Psychoanalytic Interpretation of History* (New York, 1971), p. 14.
[2] Benjamin B. Wolman *Psychoanalytic Interpretation of History* (New York, 1971), p. 84 ff.
[3] *Ibid.*, p. 89.
[4] *Ibid.*, p. 109.
[5] R. J. Lifton, *Protean Man*, p. 46 ff, in B. B. Wolman's *Psychoanalytic Interpretation of History*.

3

The Cup of Hate Runneth Over

In this chapter we shall examine some of Erasmus' anti-semitic statements in his letters, in his *Colloquies*, and in his *Ratio* — the Erasminian Methodology. From these samples we shall see that he feared Jews as dirty conspirators, that he was unable to take a consistent historical view of them, and that his propaganda against them even included labeling his Christian enemies as Jews.

Erasmus by his own testimony wrote some three thousand letters. P. S. Allen, the English historian, collected, systematized and annotated all of his Latin letters and, by the time of his death, had translated three of the eleven volumes into English.[1] Thus through Erasmus' letters we can fathom the true character of the Humanist. They are indeed revealing — particularly of his attitudes toward the Jews and Judaism. One thing is certain: we moderns know by now that it is human nature to attack savegely what one fears the most. And Erasmus was no exception.

In an early letter, Erasmus lauded the French people for keeping their country *judenrein* — Jew-proof; it was the only one of all countries in Europe that was "free from heretics, Bohemian schismatics, Jews and half-Jewish Marranos (*semi-Judeis Maranis*).[2] A few days later, he addressed himself to his friend Wolfgang Capito, the Strassburg Reformer, expressing deep concern that, with the revival of the Hebrew language, Judaism itself could be revived. And he continued: "There is nothing more hostile and dangerous for Christ's teachings than this pest."[3]

35

Returning to the same subject one year later, Erasmus was still rankled by the fact that his friend, Fabricius Capito, showed too much dedication to Hebrew studies instead of the pursuit of Greek, and he followed this up by saying: "This People, with their shudder-arousing stories, distribute, as I see it, nothing but evil stench through their Talmud, the Kabbala, the Tetragrammaton,[4] the Portals of Light [*Porta Lucis*] and other empty names. There are many Jews in Italy, and in Spain hardly any Christians. I fear that under those circumstances this erstwhile suppressed Pestilence could raise its ugly head. Besides, the Christian Church should not put so much stress upon the Old Testament." In other words, Erasmus urges his readers to slight the study of the Old Testament and advises them to clear the air of this menacing people.

What bothered Erasmus is that there were untold Christian families in Spain who before and during the Inquisition[5] had intermarried to such an alarming degree that mixing affected not only the "purity" of the Spanish people's bloodstream but had touched even the clergy and religious. "In Spain and Portugal there are monasteries and convents full of Jews. Not a few conceal Judaism in their heart and feign Christianity on account of wordly goods. Some of these feel the strings of conscience and escape, if they are able. In this city, [Amsterdam] and in several other places, we have monks, Augustinians, Franciscans, Jesuits, Dominicans, who have rejected idolatry. There are bishops in Spain and grave monks, whose parents, brothers, or sisters, dwell here [in Amsterdam] and in other cities in order to be able to profess Judaism."[6] One other way to cleanse the air would be to destroy the book-tools of the Jews, including the Old Testament, thus depriving Jews and non-Jews alike of possible means of religious if not intellectual fraternization. And this in the light of Humanism! Erasmus knew the significance of Jewish literature as a means of Jewish survival, yet it is unlikely that he understood either their true value and importance since his own Hebrew was abysmally poor.

To Johannes Schlechta, a friend in Bohemia, he wrote: "That Jews live in your country, *that* you have in common with the rest of Germany and Italy, but foremost with Spain."[7] Or to his friend Bartolini: "France alone has not been infected by heretics ... or by Jews."[8] And lastly, in the *Complaint of Peace:* "Nowhere enjoy the laws such respect, nowhere is Religion more undiminished, and not spoiled through the intercourse with Jews, as in Italy. . . ."[9] Erasmus sees in the coexistence of Jews and Gentiles a danger for the Church. He would much rather see the Jews separated, if not cast out altogether, from their symbiosis with his own kind, the pure Christians. The implication is clear: once the Jews were evicted, peace and progress could come to Christianity.

In a letter to the Dominican Prior in Cologne, Jacob Hochstraten, Erasmus rips into his close friend Johannes Reuchlin: "Reuchlin deals with nothing else but that the Jews should not suffer any injustice. Why waste so much effort to make the Jews hated? Is there anyone amongst us who does not curse this species of mankind enough? If it is Christian to hate the Jews, are we then not all Christians in over-abundance?"[10] In other words, Erasmus is puzzled by Reuchlin's humanist approach to the Jews: he simply does not hate with a vengeance. To Reuchlin a Jew is a human being, not a lesser sub-species. Erasmus sees in the Catholic hierarchy — despite his own misgivings about their inner corruption and immorality — the religious bastion against all perverters, including innovators or reformers. This being so, even a profoundly decent Christian such as Reuchlin ought to be reprimanded, if not punished, for his pro-Jewish attitudes. His bewilderment with Reuchlin evokes a perfectly self-rationalized justification to betray his friend, not to his face, but before the eager Inquisitors.

In the dedication of his *Commentary* to the Gospel of St. John, Erasmus revealed some knowledge of Jewish customs and ritual, though we must assume that he never defiled himself by attending Jewish religious worship services (otherwise he would have mentioned it, loquacious as he was): "Although the religion of the Jews can be viewed rightly as empty and false, yet they treat their Book of Law (Torah) with curious veneration, spreading it upon the purest of linen, prostate themselves before it and worship it, yet touch it only with thoroughly cleansed hands. By the same token, they godlessly disrespect, that which the Law prescribes in the first place. Thus we too must take great care not to become pious worshipers of the Gospel through ceremonials, though not be found as godless because of our non-compliance.

What then is the purpose of a book, adorned with ivory, silver, gold, silks and precious stones [an allusion to the Torah mantles], if our lives in their vulgarity are not mindful of our sins, which the Gospel abhors?"[11]

Aside from the fact that Erasmus regarded Judaism as shallow and meaningless, he was nevertheless puzzled by the supreme and exalted position the Torah enjoyed among the Jews. He admired their great loving veneration and care for it, yet he called them pests and full of sin. But with unwitting irony, he utilized Jewish symbolism to drive home a Christian homily, a preachment to his fellow Christians: What good is a fancy Good Book unless you use it and live by it? As we have seen, he urged that outward forms of reverence such as the Jews' for their Torah should betoken an inward state.

In the wake of the Lutheran Reformation came religious unrest and Erasmus hated war, especially hostility between Christians. By the same token, he dissociated himself, as Luther did, from the rebellious peasants. There was indeed a shortage of money in the fifteenth and sixteenth centuries. Governments with war debts debased coinage while taxes became oppressive. The lower classes bore the brunt and became restless when the Lords tried to retain their bondsmen or to impose seignorial obligations upon the free peasants. "Liberty and Serfdom did not make good bedfellows," to quote Lewis Spitz. In the following reign of terror many of the gentry were slain, revolutionary ideologies, coupled with anti-clericalism, were fed to the masses by roving preachers, leading to the eventual granting of greater rights to the peasants, but also to sectarianism and heresies. Erasmus, like Luther, misunderstood the peasants' economic motives, but Erasmus had his own odd theories about the causes of unrest and hostility. He gave the Peasant Revolt a sexual motivation. "The peasants" — he said — "are aiming at unbridled license to indulge their fleshly lusts, squander their inheritance in gambling and fornication." Erasmus, reflecting the medieval church's prejudices against sex, regarded the sex-act as a dirty business. He himself hated dirt and with it the "dirty farmer." Being a defender of the Church, he insisted that she remain clean, untouched by any kind of uncleanliness, physical or spiritual. Although both he and Luther spoke out

The Cup of Hate Runneth Over

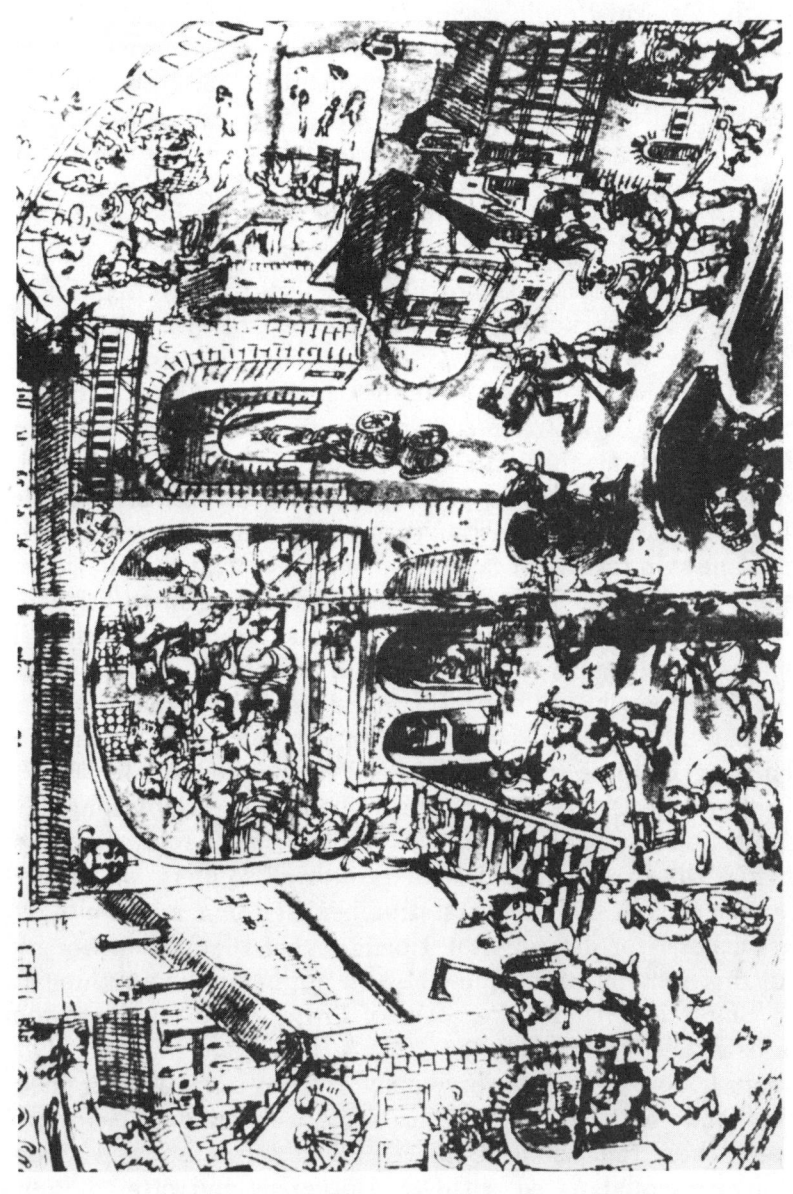

Peasants Plunder Monastery. Chronicle of Abbot Muirer of Eisenach, 1525.

against the Peasant Revolt, each reformer criticized it for different reasons. Luther saw in the Peasant Revolt a dangerous attack against Law and Order. Therefore, the disorders had to be crushed mercilessly. For Erasmus on the other hand, the dirty peasants had to be reeducated and their sex-life brought under the control of the Church, the restraining instrument against licentiousness and promiscuity. The Church, all-powerful and omniscient, was capable of preventing "dirty" human excesses of any kind. Here we must ask the question: was not Erasmus' attitude a reflection of his inner problems? Let us ask, was the fear of dirt a feeling of guilt? Was sex to him truly a sin, something that his antagonist Martin Luther resolved in a positive manner, marrying a former nun? And what was Erasmus' attitude toward fornication, and why? We will come back to this issue a little later on. Both, peasants and Anabaptists, according to Erasmus, were responsible for the polarization of Christianity into believers and rebels. But he went one step further. Erasmus smelled a plot. It was the Jews, he believed, who were secretly setting Christian against Christian. His was a primitive outcry against the "satanic power of Internal Jewry" which prays for the doom of Christianity. Contemporaries of the Hitler era will find this most revealing. This is what Erasmus had to say: "It appears to me that many Jews and Pagans are participating in these tumults [of the Peasants and Anabaptists]. The former hate Christ, the latter do not believe in anything."[12] And nine weeks later he wrote in the same vein: "In the meanwhile the earth is filled with hordes of soldiers, who spare neither friend nor foe. A great number of them are reputedly either Lutheran or Jewish. But I believe that they are unworthy even of this nomenclature, since they do not believe in anything at all."[13] Similarly: "Under the cover of Protectors of the Faith the world is filled with plunder. Spain has many secret Jews [Marranos], and Germany very many who by nature, or trained by war, tend toward robbery. This scum will inundate Germany first and then the whole Orbit."[14] That Jews showed open sympathy or collaborated with the Lutherans and offered their "fighting prowess" to the Peasants to destroy the Unity of Christendom, is pure fiction. The Jews had enough troubles of their own; they did not need warring Christian allies.

Von Koerber has pointed out[15] that Erasmus, despite his humanistic flair, suspected International Jewry of democratic tendencies which were aimed against the hierarchic structure of the Church and her monopoly of the True Faith. Beyond that he feared that the Christian multitudes were too stupid to resist this cunning plan; and since they tended to be rebellious anyhow, they accepted Jewish and non-Catholic leadership.

Koerber formulated his thoughts this way: "It appeared to him [Erasmus] that many Jews and Pagans intermingled during these highly confusing times of whom one group hated Christ, the other did not believe in anything. He suspected that the Jews had some kind of democratic ideas in mind and that behind this whole affair highly cunning plans were hidden — plans, indeed, whose originator nobody could possibly imagine up till now. Erasmus' conviction that the people were stupid, inclined to riot, and therefore in no position to exercise law and order within the State, points to the fact that his conceptualization of the State was certainly not democratically oriented." Already in his *Education of a Christian Prince* Erasmus expressed similar thoughts. To him, the Jews had been already earlier in their own history a warlike people. God himself made them this way. He was the God of Vengeance (*nakom*, in Psalm 94:1 and *Jerem.* 51:56), a Jewish Crusader-God: "The Jews were permitted to go to war, but only according to God's plan."[16] However, the Prince "should learn that the battles and butcheries of the Jews, the barbarities against their enemies are to be regarded as symbolic, otherwise the reading of these happenings could only be ruinous [to him, the Prince]."[17] Yes, the books of the Jews simply "teem" with bloody catastrophies, which an educated and a true Christian may best know how to interpret. But such a Christian will grant them no present right to conspire and fight against Christian unity. Reading further, we run into this Erasmian observation: "The Jews heard the sound of the trumpets, which permitted them to go to war. This coincides with God's sign, permitting them to hate the enemy."[18] So, what was true yesteryear, is also true today. Jews hate Christians. Let us hate the Jews now and forever.

To obtain the full measure of Erasmus' anti-Semitism, one ought to reread Erasmus' *Theological Methodology (Ratio)*, a veritable cesspool of hate. But first, let us hear again the voice of Welzig, one of the few true critics of Erasmus today: "The violence [of Erasmus] of the verbalized theological anti-semitism below is in this context not justified. Erasmus seemingly remains purposely silent regarding the theme 'Acceptance and Rejection' of the Messiah namely that the first believers of Christ belonged to the 'tricky tribe' altogether. From the western Church-fathers, such as Augustine, Erasmus could not have learned his anti-Jewish writings."[19] What makes Welzig's statement so interesting is that he uses the term "theological anti-semitism" at first but then simply concludes that Erasmus' attitude toward the Jews cannot be regarded as anything but plain, unadulterated antisemitism. It is for this reason that the reader is invited to read Erasmus' *Theological Methodology (Ratio)*. His theology is certainly not systematic but pours forth with hateful abandon. "Christ," he said, "knew the hard-heartedness (*Herzenshaerte*) of His own people which was removed from justice, so much so that it was puffed up with the conceit of false justice. He knew that it was an exceedingly tricky tribe (*raenkevoll*)." Following the medieval trend of thought, Erasmus further said that Jesus was of course maltreated and persecuted by the Jew Herod. Erasmus conveniently hid the fact that Herod was an Idumean, at best a half-Jew, and of Arab-Bedouin descent. The Jews certainly did not claim him as one of their own. And in his *Colloquies* Erasmus struck a similar theme: "Aulus. 'Do you believe that He [Jesus] was really seized by the Jews, bound, assailed and beaten, spit upon, mocked, scourged under Pontius Pilate, and finally nailed to a cross and there died?' Barb. 'I do indeed.'"[20] Erasmus continued: "He remained on the cross during their [Jews'] reviling diatribes, but He did not wish to be pitied by the women who accompanied Him. Meanwhile, He fled the multitude as if seized with disgust...." And Erasmus asked this rhetorical question, as if Jews had been avid subscribers of his polemical pamphlets: "How do you feel here in this moment, you unlucky Jew?" He added mockingly: "And you argue against your Savior without faith for whom you have waited already for so many centuries...." "Hear now, you avaricious Jew!..." For several pages the Jews were told the stories about the apostles and the doubting Thomas in

The Cup of Hate Runneth Over 43

Burning of the Jews at Trent, 1475. From a German woodcut, late 15th Century.

particular. After all he too had "descended from the exceedingly criminal, stiff-necked and revolutionary people of the Jews."[21] Erasmus then, quite typically, suddenly turned to a diminuendo mood: "For whatever the Jews were commanded to do, forbidden or permitted, is not to be applied to the life of a Christian. It is not that there was something in the books of the Old Testament that did not concern us, but that most of it was handed down at a given time as a type, disguising the coming events." What Erasmus was saying or implying was this: Historical events are always to be understood as an expression in time and space; whatever happened in those dark days of a Roman-occupied Judea with all the tragedies that ensued — including the death of Jesus and perhaps thousands of his fellow Jews — these events are not applicable for today; those things could not happen in an enlightened, humanistic age. Was not Erasmus admitting that his anti-semitic mockeries and similes were nothing else but allegorical and polemical exercises? How else could we understand him as he continued in the same breath: "...and it would be dangerous, not to regard them as allegorical." Yet they were useful to Erasmus. Or at least to the sixteenth-century reader, primarily the theological student and the intellectual. This attitude of Erasmus went well beyond what we have called heretofore ambiguity or an expression of sickness. It was a studied, tendentious ambiguity; it was propaganda. It was dangerous then, as it would be dangerous in our times.

From this new vantage-point, Erasmus' antisemitism assumes broader dimensions. He admitted to it in so many words. It was his lance that, while it once "pierced the body of Christ," now protected him by an attack upon the Savior's own people. It revealed Erasmus' awareness of his own maliciousness. And he was not ashamed to admit it inadvertently. To return to his *Ratio* and his favorite theme, he recalled how Jesus "whipped the horde of shopkeepers out of the Temple,"[22] but he then suddenly excused his Master for using ill-tempered language to the Canaanites: "He speaks at times from a strange mental attitude, when he says: It is not good to take the bread of the children and to throw it before dogs.[23] He said that by using the language of the Jews who regarded themselves as alone holy amongst mankind. However, the Canaanites, the Samaritans and other profane peoples Erasmus

The Cup of Hate Runneth Over

Caricature Showing Medieval English Jews. Exchequer Issue Roll, 1233. Public Record Office, London.

viewed as unholy and as dogs, while in the case of Jesus no discriminating differentiation of a person's national origin could have existed.[24]

While Erasmus admitted that Jesus' seemingly strange similes can only be understood in time and space, he interpreted them homiletically when aiming his volleys against the Jews, calling *them* racist and therefore unholy. Did Erasmus not know that the Jews had excluded the Samaritans from the rebuilding of the Temple, once they had returned from their exile, because they had intermarried with pagans while Jews themselves in Babylon had remained God's people? Did Erasmus not know that exclusion was strictly for reasons of self-preservation as a People, and that half-Jews could have alienated the Jews from a faithful adherence to the Law? Did Erasmus not know that it was the *Siyog la-Torah*, the fence around the Torah, that had been Israel's life-preserver ever since the days of the Great Prophets? Racism was alien to Jewish tradition. "Are not the Ethiopians my people also?" the Old Testament asks.

Similarly, we can detect this almost sick irrationalism in his letter to Ammonius in which he regretted that the Jewish physician to Pope Julius II did not use hellbore to cure him from his madness.[25] Considering that this plant had an offensive smell and was used as a parasiticide (it belongs to the Crowfoot family), one wonders reading the Greek which concealed meaning from the prying eye, if Erasmus was not alluding to both the Jew *and* the Pope. He wrote: "And yet I know not *whom* to blame, unless it be that circumcised chief-priest's [the Pope's] physician, who is either no artist, or else both Anticyras are used up. But I trust the fates themselves will find a way." The Humanist closed his *Ratio* with an almost bizarre prayer: "We therefore must pray to Christ that he either change this brood of Pharisees for the better or chase them from his herd. This is said not to insult the good Jews (who may convert) but to remind the bad ones of their duty."[26]

During the days when the publisher Aldus Manutius was collaborating with Erasmus, Aleander, the Italian humanist, was his confidant. Years later Aleander suspected Erasmus of being a secret fellow traveller in the cause of the Reformation. But Erasmus had a ready alibi: "I don't know Luther, neither have I

The Cup of Hate Runneth Over

Disputation between Jewish and Christian Scholars. From a woodcut from Seelenwurzgarten, 1483.

read his writings," he said. Yet, few people believed him. As a consequence, Aleander accused Erasmus of being foxy and cunning. The latter fought back, and "he did not shy away from the use of the most highly questionable means."[27] In a letter, dated December, 1520, Erasmus — exploiting the general hostility against the Jews — now called his former friend a Jew. He wrote: "One thing is sure: despite the papal edict the Bulla against Luther was published. Aleander, who presented it, said, he had no other order but to negotiate with the Universities exclusively. There is a man, who understand the three languages (Greek, Latin and Hebrew) — and as all say: he is a Jew."[28]

In this way, Erasmus hoped to get even with the papal nuntius (ambassador), now his enemy. Rereading the *Acta Academiae Lovaniensis* we can find these invectives: "...that he [Aleander] was born a Jew, but whether he had been baptized, nobody knew. However, he was certainly not a Pharisee, for he did not believe in the resurrection of the dead." And to prove his contention that Aleander was a Jew, he cited his obvious Jewish character traits in a letter to Willibald Pirckheimer (3/30/1522) as bombastic, "arrogant, irritable and of insatiable cupidity for glory and profit."[29] Erasmus showed the same hatred, though covered with satire, against Pope Julius II in his *Julius Exclusus* (from Heaven) in which he also implied that the Pope was of Jewish descent — only to disassociate himself later on from the authorship. W. P. Eckert, the author of a two volume work on Erasmus, asked whether "this man from Rotterdam [was] not very scrupulous with the truth?"[30]

Only five months later (8/8/1522), Erasmus, riled by a literary attack of Jacob Lopez Stunica, who criticized him for his poor translation of the Greek New Testament as exegetical and his plagiarism, accused his friend also of being a Jew who "plays in Rome the same monkish role as Pfefferkorn played while in Cologne."[31] Luther, later on, was to find himself also in the same company of crypto-Jews, such as Stunica and Aleander. In this case it was not guilt by association, a technique which Erasmus so often used, but intellectual guilt: these men, in his opinion, acted and talked as if they were Jews.[32] Erasmus regarded Luther as a crypto-Jew. (Conversely, Luther, upon hearing of the defeat of the

The Cup of Hate Runneth Over

Church in the Shallows of Heresy.

Imperial Marshal von Katzian by the Turks, suspected that the Marshal was born a Jew.)[33]

During his correspondence with Johannes Reuchlin, Erasmus took issue with his literary friend regarding the *Augenspiegel*, the tract against Pfefferkorn. In a letter dated from Basel, August, 1514, Erasmus wrote: "I read your apologia, fresh, confident, brilliant, eloquent, sharp and written too eruditely. There is only one thing I miss, dear Capnio [Reuchlin], I speak frankly and in friendship, I would have much rather seen, that you, instead of using greater brevity in common places, had not gone off on a tangent, and had not avoided punchy invectives" (against the Jews).[34]

What Erasmus was saying here is simple: he missed in Reuchlin's self-defense, in which he eventually moved to the offensive against Pfefferkorn and the bigoted Inquisitors, the same kind of ugly language he himself used against Jews. Erasmus' hate-mongering was premeditated and not solely an expression of a sick body and mind. K. H. Rengstorf, feeling embarrassed by his humanist idol, makes this comment: "Such expressions coming from the mouth of a superior man betray only too clearly how deeply the aversion against Jews had already gone, and that it did not even stop in the face of a Convert. . . ."[35] By contrast, this writer wishes to offer his readers a different view, of Raymond Lullus for instance,[36] a humanist dreamer of a Universal Religion (1235-1315). In his *Book of The Pagan and the Three Wise Men*, the author allowed the Pagan to discuss the religions of Christianity, Judaism, and Islam with three respective exponents. The savants agreed in the belief in one God and Salvation. However, they could not agree among themselves which the true religion really was. Yet, they held that the day would come when the truth would be found in an atmosphere of brotherly harmony. Small wonder that the famous German playwright Gotthold Ephraim Lessing (1729-81) in his play *Nathan der Weise* two hundred years later used Lullus' humanist characters in his efforts to reeducate the frustratingly prejudiced German masses of his own time.

In sharp contrast to Erasmus, a final voice ought to be heard, a voice that managed to sing a hymn of pious dignity in an age of transition — a dignity with the inner strength to regard man as man, irrespective of his Faith. The voice belonged to Rabbi Yom Tov Lipman, an educated Jewish Humanist of his time.

"Christians ask us whether we have proselytes.... If a bad Jew allows himself to become baptized, he does it ... to shake off the yoke of the Heavenly Realm.... He believes himself free from all commandments and in so doing makes himself into a slave of evil and leads an easy life.... The Proselytes, however, who convert to us, come [to us] out of the use of their own free will into servitude, from light into darkness. Men know full well that they must become circumcised, that they must wander restlessly from one place to the other, that they deprive themselves from the gratification of all good things, that their lives are threatened by the gentiles and that they say farewell to all delights. Likewise the women who wish to enter the community of Jews, must surrender all the pleasantries and pleasures of life. And yet, despite it all, there are always proselytes who flee to the protective wings of the divine Majesty...."[37]

Erasmus' contradictory and paradoxical attitudes toward his friends and foes as expressed in his letters, and to his contemporaries, have many modern scholars baffled. Cornelis Reedijk wrote: "It becomes increasingly difficult to form a clear picture of his character."[38] But the man who really poured cold water upon that "tragic man"[39] was none other than Henry Osborn Taylor, who said some forty years ago: "Had Erasmus written less, he might be more read today. His writings are not needed now!"[40] These critiques also embrace Erasmus' warped sentiments against the Jews of his time.

To sum up, one more word ought to be said about Erasmus' inner malaise as it reflected itself in his outward behavior toward the Jews. It cannot be emphasized too strongly that, what we call today antisemitism, was at the time of this remarkable man part and parcel of Christian theology, an integral part of every Christian's daily vocabulary and the inevitable by-product of the Church's competitive and missionary character. The Jew was the tempter, a sub-human cretain which God allowed the Church to survive as the witness for the death of Christ, actually and symbolically. This was the main theme of Christian education. Erasmus and Luther both had inherited this ideology and —

believed it. However, Christian Humanists in their day made a desperate attempt to reassess its traditional position. Certainly not to give up wholly its anti-Jewish tradition and vocabulary, but to dare come up with a more humane approach toward an understanding and worth of Jewish writings, including the Bible, but also to re-evaluate the individual Jew as to what he represented in actual life. The thinking, moderate humanist rejected the fanatical concept that the Jew was totally bad, satanic and to be held in constant readiness for his extirpation or expulsion. And so, as we look at these men, we come up with an interesting conclusion: Erasmus, working for the Restoration of the Old Faith and Luther for the Reformation of the Mother Church, showed one common bond, their undying enmity of the Jews. In this respect their so-called Humanism remained truly within the deep fold of medieval Christian thinking and feeling. In the case of Erasmus, it did not make any difference to him, the *inner* man, whether a good man or name was hurt. What mattered was much more compelling: his heart declared war against the enemies of Christ. His psyche needed it for self-protection. In all of his work he battled against Christ's enemies, and with his pen he crucified them—just as *they* had done to Him centuries ago. His fanatical love for Christ went, therefore, way beyond the missionary: as if in an act of transference, Christ became his Father in lieu of his real father he had never known. And he clung to him with all the obsession and fervor of a child which dreads rejection or punishment. He showed himself as medieval as Luther, including the mystical overtones of his thoughts. After all, he had been trained by the Dutch Brethren of the Common Life. Now we understand why he raved and ranted against the Pelagians, Arians, Carthusians, Turks, Manichaeans, and Jews all his life. It were they who endangered his Father. And so it came from his own lips: "Nihil nobis cum Judaeis" — "We have nothing to do with the Jews," he said in his *Diatribe*. He had rejected them outwardly and inwardly. This suffering servant of the Lord.

NOTES

[1] Werner Welzig did the same for German scholars.
[2] W. Welzig, *Erasmus Letters* Vol. II, 501, pp. 11 ff. Marranos are crypto-Jews who converted to Christianity under duress (death, expulsion and/or confiscation of property). Many of them practiced their faith secretly, living a double life. The Church watched them closely and showed little mercy when Marranos were apprehended and brought before the Tribunal.
[3] The four-letter mystical and ineffable name of God.
[4] On another occasion, repeating himself and using the same phraseology, he added: "I had rather see Christ infected by Scotus than by that rubbish."
[5] These tribunals were established in the Middle Ages. Originally, the condemnation of heretics (disbelievers from the orthodox point of view) was entrusted to the Lombard bishops in 1183 by the Council of Verona, which may be said to have laid the foundation of the Inquisition, particularly severe and merciless in Spain. If a heretic refused to recant, the ecclesiastical authorities handed him over to the civil authorities to be dealt with. This search and destroy mission of the Church was first put into effect in Languedoc (France) against the Albigensians. From there it spread little by little over the Christian World. Used during its early stages against secret Jews (Marranos) and Moslems (Moriscos), it served also to discourage Catholic desertions. The rationale behind the death penalty for heretics was somewhat ironic: the Church believed that by killing a dissenter, it would shorten his sinful life here on earth and thus aggravate his stay in purgatory.
[6] Heinrich Grätz, quoting an eyewitness. *History of the Jews*, Vol. V (Philadelphia, 1941), p. 91.
[7] Welzig, Vol. IV, 114, pp. 44-46.
[8] Epistle 599, Antwerp 3/10/1516.
[9] Welzig, p. 403.
[10] Welzig, Vol. IV, 46 pp. 138-143.
[11] Welzig, Vol. V, 168 ff, pp. 223-231.
[12] Welzig, Vol. VIII, 1131, pp. 215-217.
[13] *Ibid.*, 194, pp. 59-63.
[14] Welzig, Vol. IX, 243, pp. 24-28.
[15] Von Koerber, *Die Staatstheorie des Erasmus von Rotterdam* (Berlin, 1967), p. 43.
[16] Welzig, Vol. V, p. 353.
[17] *Ibid.*, p. 249.
[18] W. Welzig, *Die Klage des Friedens*, Vol. V., pp. 383, 385; and Letter # 590.
[19] W. Welzig, Erasmus' *Ratio*, p. 339.
[20] C. R. Thompson, *The Colloquies of Erasmus* (Chicago, 1965), p. 183.
[21] *Ibid.*, pp. 231-255.
[22] *Ibid.*, pp. 18, 185, 181.
[23] Erasmus quotes here from Matthew 15:26 in his *Ratio* (W. Welzig edition).
[24] This is how W. Welzig characterizes Erasmus' attitude.

[25] Letter to his friend Ammonius, Cambridge, Nov. 11, 1511. Incidentally, Anticyra was a small town in Phocia, Greece. It was famous for its black hellebore, an herb regarded also as a cure against insanity.

[26] Erasmus' closing statement in his *Ratio*, p. 495.

[27] W. P. Eckert, *Erasmus von Rotterdam, Werk und Wirkung*, Vol. II (Cologne, 1967), pp. 345.

[28] P. S. Allen, Erasmus' *Letters* #170 (Oxford, 1906-47).

[29] *Ibid.*, p. 346 ff.

[30] *Ibid.*, p. 346.

[31] R. Friedenthal, *Luther, Sein Leben und Seine Zeit* (Munich, 1971), p. 644. Pfefferkorn, the infamous Jewish convert who sold out to the Dominicans.

[32] Luther wrote once: And if I had been a Jew, and seen such stupidity and such blockheads reign in the Christian Church, I would have rather been a pig than a Christian.... I beg you therefore my deal Papists, if you become tired of abusing me as a heretic, that you begin to revile me as a Jew!" Erasmus deduced from that that Luther was of Jewish descent!

[33] Friedenthal, p. 650.

[34] Erasmus' *Letters*, ed. by W. Koehler, Vol. II, pp. 224-227 (New Edition by A. Flitner, Dietrich Collect., Bremen 1956, #73, p. 109.)

[35] K. H. Rengstorf, *Kirche and Synagoge*, Vol. 1 (Stuttgart, 1968), p. 284.

[36] A mystic from the Island of Majorca.

[37] K. H. Rengstorf, p. 254.

[38] C. Reedijk, *What is Typically Dutch in Erasmus?* (New York, 1960), p. 25.

[39] R. Friedenthal, p. 130.

[40] Taylor, *Thought and Expression in the Sixteenth Century* (New York, 1930), Vol. I, p. 160.

4

The Betrayal of Reuchlin and Friends

During the late fifteenth and sixteenth centuries Germany was a highly conservative, moral, and Christian country, while the Romance lands such as Spain, France, and Italy were already infected by what can be called the Renaissance Mood. It bred moral corruption, over-refinement, and in part non-Christian attitudes. The new accent was on a fuller expression of all facets of secular life, contrasting with the family-based religiosity of the people to the North. And because the Germans "had retained their original Teutonic dullness,"[1] their humorless way of life was threatened by this new germ which had already crept across the Alps. A scapegoat, had to be found, so they thought, guilty of having corrupted the whole of the Christian world. The avant-guardists of the Cross, the Dominicans in Cologne, became the shock-troops in this battle to keep the Church free from foreign influences. Since they were too insignificant in numbers to take on the whole of this infected new world, the Jews offered a convenient sacrificial lamb. How to fight this enemy of Christendom was the question. Herr Hoogstraten (Hochstraten), Arnold of Tongern, and Ortuinus (Ortuin) Gratius became the Church's inquisitors to take on the helpless Jews. What better ally could these men wish for to defeat the arch-enemy of Christendom than one of their own people? For there were baptized Jews around who for opportunism or for reasons of "guilt" wished to sell out their own former kin. There was Victor von Karben, an ignorant apostate, who claimed that Jewish writings, such as the Talmud and the Kabbala, were full of anti-Christian teachings, sneering at its Teacher and Founder. He advised the hebraically illiterate inquisitors to have the Jewish writings burned. He had three reasons: Jews practice usury, so he said; they could not be forced to go to Church; and they were attached to their secret book, the Talmud. Once the Talmud was removed, Jews could be forced in their helplessness to embrace the new faith, Christianity. However, the Dominicans soon found a better subject, the ex-Jew Pfefferkorn, a former butcher and convicted thief. To ingratiate himself with the clerics, he allowed his name to be used on a series of pamphlets, hastily concocted and distributed all over Western Germany to discredit the Jews and provoke riots and bloodshed. After the confiscation of the Talmud, Jews could then be threatened with conversion or, if they still resisted, with expulsion. At first, the Dominican ruse did not cause much of a ripple.

Actually the German masses were disinterested in theological issues. They had met Jewish converts indeed, but their brotherly love or antipathy was not kindled by their presence. Embarrassed, they, as well as the threatened Jews, denounced Pfefferkorn. His *A Mirror for Admonition* (1507), and Gratius' *The Enemy of the Jews* were circulated (1509). The old anti-Jewish calumnies were repeated and a new one added: Jewish doctors had plotted the death of their Christian patients. Gratius again demanded the confiscation and public burning of the Talmud and beyond that the robbing of Jewish properties for the enrichment of the Church. Emperor Maximilian, at first wary of Dominican intrigues, eventually lent an ear to his sister, Kunigunde—the "sinful" daughter of Emperor Frederick, who had wound up in a Franciscan convent. This superstitious and gloomy divorcee of Duke Albert of Munich, allowed Pfefferkorn an interview during which he again accused the Jews of treason, murder, theft, and other crimes. Shocked and perplexed, she believed him, and in a letter to her brother called for a stop to Jewish infamy. Pfefferkorn then travelled to Italy where, on August 19, 1509, he secured an imperial mandate: "Examine the Hebrew books for manifestations of anti-Christian bias—and that without Jewish resistance!"[2] Frankfort, the seat of Talmudic learning and of rich

The Betrayal of Reuchlin and Friends 57

Jews Wearing Badge Taking the Oath *More Judaico.* From a German woodcut, 1509.

Jews, was his first stop. Prayerbooks were confiscated, Jewish services forbidden, and the feast of Succoth (Booths) outlawed by the apostate himself and before the assemblage of all Jews, clergy, and members of the Senate.

The Jews resisted the confiscation and a house-to-house search. They protested to Uriel von Gemmingen, the kind Archbishop of Mainz. Upon his intercession, Pfefferkorn and the Senate were rebuked. Indirectly, the Dominicans also were checked. The Jews began to mobilize public opinion. Uriel then sent a letter to the Emperor with the request to have experts examine the questionable Hebrew writings. He also wrote to the humanist knight Ulrich von Hutten, the brilliant friend of Erasmus, at that time his agent at the Imperial Court.

Reuchlin, who held an honorific title given to him by Emperor Maximilian, Triumvir of the Swabian League, and the ex-Jew Victor von Karben were asked to impartially examine the books. Reuchlin at that time was already the recognized intellectual "pride of Germany," a defender of Hebrew and advocate of the study of Hebrew for scientific propagation of the Faith. It was Reuchlin's plan to understand the Old Testament writings in their original uncorrupt fashion and to help Jews to make the transition from their old Faith to the New Faith. This was in keeping with the Catholic tradition as pronounced at the Council of Vienna in 1311. Petrus Negri (Peter Schwarz), the first antisemitic Hebrew scholar and teacher at the University of Ingolstadt (around 1470), also tried to utilize Hebrew to lead Jews to the baptismal fountain. He had authored the first Hebrew textbook Kokhav haMashiakh (Stella Mashiakh, in 1477) from which the Humanist K. Pellican had studied. In those days the study of Hebrew was not a labor of love, but a theological snare devised for the conversion of the Jews. Yet, it is interesting to note that these theological propagandists utilized Hebrew scholars as their "silent partners" (but never openly admitted as their teachers) — who received only vilification once they had done their duty.

Reuchlin himself had the peaceful, humanist approach to learning, not the bloody kind of the inquisitor-theologians.[3] Following in the footsteps of Pico, he consulted Jewish, Christian, and Platonic authors, with no other desire but "to raise the hearts of men to God, that is to bring them close to perfect bliss. . . . Whoever devotes his entire work and effort to this end, acquires happiness in this life, eternal joy in that (other; namely Heaven)." As it turned out, the choice of Reuchlin as an impartial judge on the Committee sparked an explosion, the reverberations of which were heard from one end of Europe to the other. His life was the visible testimony of a truly great man who had made the transition from Medievalism to Modernity without compromises, as Erasmus tried but failed to do in his effort to sythesize Greek paganism with Christian orthodoxy.

Reuchlin was older than Erasmus. His mind was incisive, fair, truth-loving, and honest. By all standards he, like Bude[4] was more versatile, esthetic, and humanist not only in outlook but also in performance. Like Bileam, who came to curse the Israelites in their encampment and wound up praising their hosts, Reuchlin became so engrossed in the study of Hebrew writings that his labor turned to love; his enthusiasm was infectious. Pico della Mirandola, his Italian counterpart, in turn introduced him into the marvels of Hebrew Mysticism, the Kabbala. Reuchlin had entered into an entirely new life and world. It seems as if he had outgrown not only the Middle Ages but also his Teutonic contemporaries. At last he came under the influence of the Hebrew scholar and imperial physician, Dr. Jacob Loens. Through him Reuchlin became the leading Hebraist in Germany, mastering it like an Old Testament sage. The following words sounded like a confessional: "The language of Hebrew is simple, uncorrupted and holy, terse and vigorous. God confers in it directly with men, and men with angels, without interpreters, face to face . . . as one friend converses with another."[5] What a contrast to that ex-Jew Pfefferkorn! Back in Italy at the Court of Pope Alexander VI, Reuchlin's second teacher was Obadja Sforno. Unlike Erasmus, who felt contaminated in the presence of a Jew, Reuchlin did not mind regarding Sforno as his equal in learning and piety.

Reuchlin was not totally free from anti-Jewish bias. To him Jews were blind unbelievers, and most of the canards rampant in his time were part of his early vocabulary. However, as he matured, he came to appreciate the Jews for what they really were: human beings. "He gave them his affection, or at least his esteem ... his sense of justice did not allow him to let wrong be done to them, much less to help in doing it."[6]

Reuchlin was the most beloved of all German Humanists. Erasmus knew it and envied him. The Dominicans, not yet charging him with heretical views, sensed instinctively that Reuchlin was their enemy. After all, he was a "Hebrew Literature-Lover." By now Reuchlin himself felt endangered upon hearing that Pfefferkorn had asked the Emperor for a second mandate against the Jews. Again, some activist Jews, Jonathan Levi Zion of Frankfort and his friend and delegate at the Imperial Court, Isaac Trieste, nullified Pfefferkorn's machinations — enjoined by influential non-Jewish friends, including some political figures. Maximilian, in a fit of pettiness — after all the Jews had defied him and not surrendered all their holy books — had the old order reinstated. The Jews were told to give up their holy books: more than 1500 books were stored in the town hall of Frankfort alone. So it went throughout Germany. Many of the Princes were disgusted by this ugly show, and so were some of the Church's bishops. All of them were repelled by Pfefferkorn's intrigues — especially when another one of his pamphlets appeared, *In Praise and Honor of Emperor Maximilian*. The voices of the common man, of princes and of bishops became so noisy in time that the vacillating Maximillian had second thoughts: He rescinded the book-burning order — but not until all the Hebrew books had been cleared of subversion.

What followed were acts of desperation by the Dominican witch hunters. Renewed rumors were spread alleging Jewish kidnapping, thievery, desecration of the Host, and so on. A second Commission, composed of its former members Hochstraten and von Karben was called into session. But for the first time Reuchlin was given the mandate to state categorically and specifically if the Talmud was indeed detrimental to Christianity. This was the key issue to which the Humanist wished to address himself. His answer, despite a heavy juridical style, was favorable to the Jews. After classifying this huge legal compendium, Reuchlin categorically declared that it was indispensable to Christian theology. As a matter of fact, most of the important Christian commentators had borrowed generously from the works of the Old Testament

Desiderius Erasmus of Holland. From a sketch by Albert Dürer.

exegetists, as Rashi had been used long before him by Nicolaus of Lyra. As for the Talmud, Reuchlin saw in it the centuries-old, accumulated wealth of rational Jewish scientific thinking that was in no way distinguishable from Greek, Latin, or German works. And since the inquisitors, including Pfefferkorn, were ignorant of the subject, they could not possibly judge it fairly and truthfully. So, he concluded: "If the Talmud were deserving of such condemnation, our ancestors of many hundred years ago, whose zeal for Christianity was much greater than ours, would have burnt it. The baptized Jews, Peter Schwarz (Negri) and Pfefferkorn, the only persons who insist on its being burnt, probably wish it for private reasons."[7]

The allusion was clear: Reuchlin by implication accused the Dominicans of conspiracy. He even went one step further. With the aid of Pico della Mirandola, the Italian Humanist and Kabbalist, Reuchlin recommended that the Jews should retain full ownership of their sacred writings and that they should remain in their trust. Beyond that, he dared to propose that in all German Universities, Chairs of Hebrew Studies be established for a period of ten years, occupied by a Rabbi or learned Christian professor. This in 1510! Reuchlin's philosophy was clear: Hebrew deserved an equal place with Greek and Latin in the pursuit of classical and humanist studies, and beyond that — curious from our modern point of view — Jews were to be induced by gentle means and conviction to embrace Christianity. We can only guess whether he added this afterthought to calm the Dominicans or actually believed it himself.

Two main ideological defenses were stressed by Reuchlin: one, that the Jews as residents and members of the Holy Roman Empire had full and equal rights as citizens; and second, that the Jews should not be treated or considered as heretics since they were totally outside the Christian faith and, therefore, beyond ecclesiastical jurisdiction. Reuchlin sent his brief in a sealed package to the Archbishop Uriel by a special, duly sworn messenger. It was meant to be read by him alone and the Emperor. However, Pfefferkorn had this document intercepted and Reuchlin, justifiably irritated, implicated the Dominicans in the plot. Now on the defensive, they set out to refute Reuchlin's defense of the Jews. When a new pamphlet, *The Handspiegel* (Hand-Mirror) appeared on the streets of Germany, Reuchlin's hundreds of friends protested to Emperor Maximilian, who again promised another investigation. However, political unrest in Italy kept him from taking a decisive stand. Reuchlin in desperation issued a reply in *The Augenspiegel* (Spectacles). In it he disproved thirty-four lies which the Dominicans had committed, including the accusation that he had been bribed by the Jews to come to their aid. The following confession of Reuchlin became a classic among Humanists: "The baptized Jew [Pfefferkorn] writes that Divine law forbids our holding communion with Jews; this is not true. Every Christian may go to law with them, buy of or make presents to them. Cases may occur where Christians inherit legacies together with Jews. It is allowed to converse with and learn from them, as Saint Jerome and Nicolas de Lyra did. And lastly, a Christian should love a Jew as his neighbor; all this is founded on the Law [of Moses]." And then: "I favor the Jews in such a manner that they have not committed a crime, but that they will not suffer any injustice. The duties of simple humane association and social intercourse demand, that one does not regard even a criminal as beyond justice and treat him as such. Injustice is brutality, the disavowal of all humanity which makes one who strives after it, into a beast."[8]

The Jews were overjoyed by this statement. They bought up copies of this best-seller, which sold by the thousands at the Frankfort Fair. Reuchlin was swamped by messages of good will from all sides and the Humanists treated their hero like a saint.

However, the witch hunters rallied again and staged another kangaroo court in which Reuchlin was accused of three most grievous errors: favoring the Jews, insulting the Church, and heresy. The verdict they demanded was: to condemn, suppress, and burn the *Augenspiegel*. Had German public opinion not rallied at this juncture overwhelmingly to Reuchlin's side, it is quite possible that the Inquisitors would have burned Reuchlin upon the stake. The students of the University of Mainz (Mayence) protested in favor of Reuchlin. Reuchlin, in a moment of bitter reflection, wrote satirically that his judge was a Judas and the inquisitor an "Inquinitor," a soiler of character.[9] But Hochstraten, acting as Inquisitor and Judge both, was unperturbed by puns. However, in the midst of the "court-proceedings" a messenger presented a letter from Uriel von Gemmingen, demanding a stop and delay of this trial. In the meanwhile Reuchlin sent an urgent appeal through his friend, the Jewish papal physician Bonet de Lates, to Pope Leo X. This Pope, the wisest and shrewdest of the Medici, was a politician rather than a worthy occupant of the papal throne. He had an uncanny distrust of the Inquisition. Reuchlin's cause won a reprieve. Through much backstairs diplomacy, the trial of Reuchlin was again postponed. Archbishop Uriel even fined Hochstraten one hundred and eleven Rhenish gold florins for the slander of Reuchlin, and thus muzzled his mouth.

Germany was sent into two antagonistic camps: the united Dominican and Obscurantist axis on one side, the Humanists and their allies on the other. It was a last gasp of the intolerant Middle Ages. In this fight the fiercest defenders of Reuchlin were Ulrich von Hutten, Hermann von Busche, Crotus Rubianus, Sebastian Münster, Widmannstadt, and Egidio de Viterbo, the Kabbalist. The Dominican Front bid for time. They hoped that a venal papacy could eventually be paid off with money, and Reuchlin be impoverished due to drawn-out court actions. Whereupon they insulted the Emperor and the Pope both and even threatened to ally themselves with the Protestant Hussites in Bohemia against the Pope!

But the Reuchlinists were not idle either: knowing that the Papcy was corrupt and Maximilian a tool of his crazed sister and the crafty Dominicans, they decided to appeal directly to the German people. In a popular vein, the Humanist Rubianus ridiculed the intriguer Gratius by lampooning his poor Latin, absurd logic, foolish chatter, contemptable lust, and immorality. The German masses, although quasi-illiterate but appreciating vile language, applauded the sarcastic *Letters of Obscurantists* (1515). Recklessly, Rubianus identified the Dominicans as the product of the Catholic Church and derided the bigots and tyrants of the hierarchy. All of Europe began to laugh at this Reuchlin *vs.* Church controversy. "Erasmus also joined this humanist chorus despite his kidney ailment, but when this thing became empyreu-

The Betrayal of Reuchlin and Friends 65

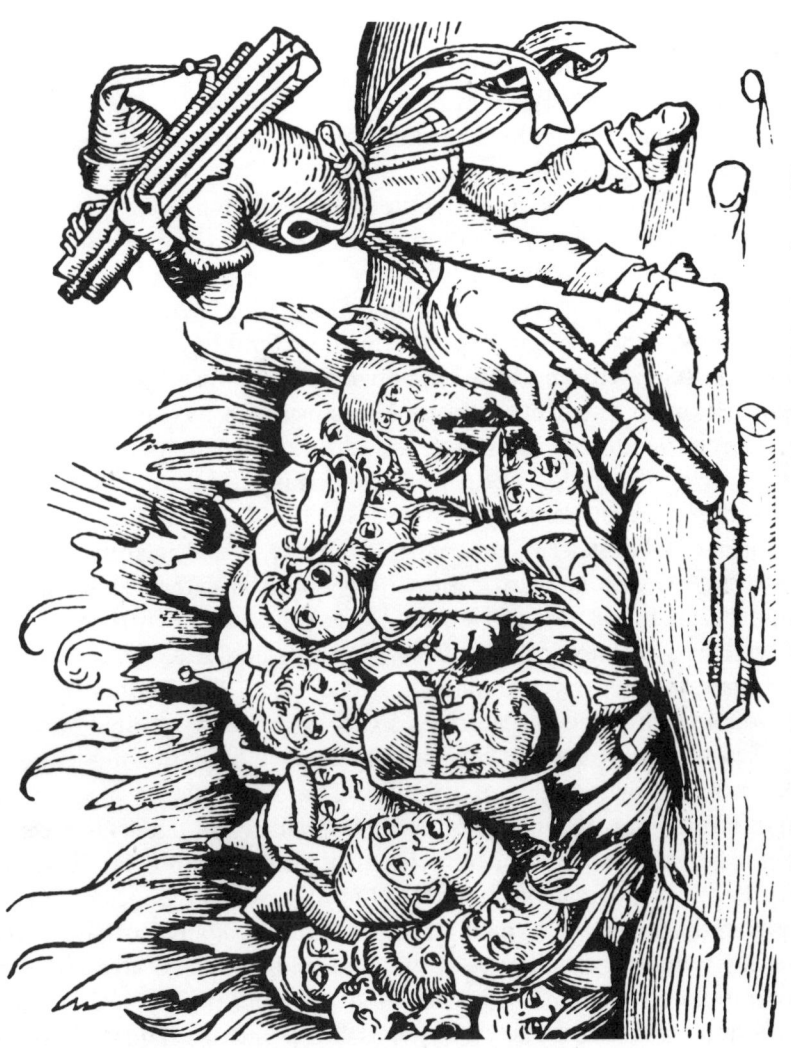

Burning of Jews. From a woodcut from Schedel's *Weltchronik*, 1493.

matic (hot!) when the attacks [against him] accumulated, he did not wish to have anything to do with this whole mess, naturally. It seemed to him compromising."[10] Nevertheless, in public opinion the Dominican case was dismissed long before the official Church verdict was out. But the Jews became apprehensive. They knew that before long, this whole intra-Christian quarrel might boomerang; and they were right. It was left to Erasmus to fan the flames of hate against the Jews again and by implication against his "friend" Reuchlin.

It is not that Erasmus wanted to be drawn into this fight or itched for one. He was simply drawn into it by a force greater than he expected. The issue at hand was Reuchlin's valiant effort to save the whole of Hebrew literature which hostile forces had confiscated and threatened to burn in public. This dangerous threat posed a tremendous challenge to Humanistic society. A few years prior to the Reformation, Erasmus had advocated freedom of speech, academic freedom, and the right of man to choose his own circle of friends without being charged by the Church as a heretic or a heretic by association. But the Reuchlin case created a dilemma. If Humanism meant free inquiry into the sources of the past, the classics and antiquity, how could any true Humanist be opposed to the study of Hebrew? It expressed the culture of Jesus as well as the ancients, be they the Mosaic Law, prophecy, the Psalmists, or history. A man like Reuchlin fully understood that by reading the ancient sources in the original a scholar could be helpful to the cause of Christianity, and would become a better and more knowledgeable Christian. There was also a moral issue. How could the Religion which preached love and compassion, even of the enemy, uphold the principles of free learning and inquiry, and in the same breath denigrate the very people who had survived hundreds of years of persecution because of these very writings which gave them knowledge and comfort, strength, and an abundance of human love for God and mankind?

Where was Erasmus? What was his position? Did he opt for Humanism or Obscurantism? Or did he remain within the fold of the Medieval Theologians? Are we privy to his utterances for or against the fight which engulfed both the Catholic Church and the Humanists? Was he a hero or a coward in this struggle which lasted

Miniature of John Colet before St. Matthew, 1509.

for a long time and which sapped the religious strength of western Europe deep into the Reformation period? There are other questions we have to ask of Erasmus. Did he at any time, consistently and forcefully, stand up for the moral and scientific issues at stake? Did he prove to be Reuchlin's friend and did he speak up for him when his friend found himself sometimes alone against the orthodox hierarchy or Inquisition? And since this struggle for Humanist Freedom involved the Jews and their survival kit, the Biblical and Talmudic Literature, what were Erasmus' reactions and reflections in the face of Jewish book-burnings?

At that time, in the Spring of 1514, Erasmus was in England. Reuchlin sat down and wrote a letter to Erasmus in which he brought him up to date on the issues. It seems that the Bishop of Speyer had permitted him to win over Erasmus and his English friends to the cause. In his reply, courteous and encouraging, Erasmus told Reuchlin that John Colet, Thomas More, John Fisher, the Bishop of Rochester, and others were in his camp to salvage the threatened Hebrew Literature from extinction. But he counselled moderation. Three more letters were exchanged between them, each friendly and expressing Victory for the Cause of Humanism. It seems that Erasmus was so overwhelmed by Reuchlin's struggle against the Dominican aggressors and their puppet, the apostate Pfefferkorn, that he called his friend Reuchlin a unique and incomparable ornament on the German scene. Thus the die was cast: Reuchlin with his progressive and learned allies were on one side, Dominican Orthodoxy on the other. On another occasion, Erasmus boasted: "Farewell," he said in a subsequent letter, "and, please count Erasmus amongst those who deep in their hearts wish you well."[11] More and more letters were exchanged. Erasmus wrote feverishly to such greats as Thomas More, Thomas Woolsey, again to John Fisher, Pirckheimer, and Banisius.

Then suddenly came the switch: Erasmus showed unhappiness and irritation that his own name had been dragged into the controversy.[12] He detested religious fights, any fight, particularly when it involved a Jew. In his now famous letter to Willibald Pirckheimer in Nuremberg he wrote:

I do not regard anything more unsavory but to always argue and fight, especially then when it involves a loathsome and unworthy adversary. Who is this man to whom Reuchlin does have to give battle? ... See here, please, what kind of a tool these pretentious teachers of the true religion use.[13] He is a shameful ignoramus, to whom to teach a lesson would not cause the slightest damage. He is not to be called a semi-iudaeus (half-Jew), since he has through his deeds proven to be a super-Jew [sesqui-iudaeus]. Even Satan himself could not have wished for himself a more effective tool, this eternal enemy of the Christian Religion, than such a person who from an angel of light changed to an angel of Satan: and all this under the pretext of the defense of Religion in order to destroy the most important achievement of our Religion, namely the Harmony of the Christian World. I should drop dead if this man did not convert for any other reason but to cause a major catastrophe amongst the Christians and, once accepted into our ranks, to infect the whole of Christianity with his Jewish gift. What could he have achieved, had he remained a Jew, since he was one anyhow?[14]

But now he proceeds in a typical Jewish manner after he has placed a Christian mantilla about his shoulders. Now he clings to his own people even the more. The Jews alone have scoffed at Christ, but this man rages against many reputable and, through their life's work and erudition, prominent men. He could not have served his own fellow-Jews better, feigning conversion, to betray the interests of Christianity to its foes: a man who otherwise is a good-for-nothing, proves ingenious in order to rise as a hostile accuser.[15]

What Erasmus is saying here is "Once a Jew, always a Jew." This showed again the ambiguity of Erasmus' Christian feelings toward the Jew: may he be damned if he converted, be damned if he did not. This whole correspondence proves that Erasmus had now unexpectedly become a target of the Dominicans, the defenders of the Mother-Church. He riled under the impact of their blows; even more so when Pfefferkorn himself singled him out for scorn, as he revealed in a letter to his friend Gerhard Lister, to whom he wrote on that very same day: "that Pfefferkorn himself has reviled me in a new book."[16] There was a further dilemma: he had been willing to defend his friend Reuchlin; he was unwilling to seem to defend Jews, on whose behalf Reuchlin had acted.

Erasmus' dilemma caused him sleepless nights; he hated to be slandered by his own Church, and on the other hand he wished to pose as a genuine Humanist. His cowardliness to take an open and forthright stand in favor of progress caused him to bury his head. But there was no escape. For years men of progress had to witness this spectacle of a reluctant Humanist driven to desperation, pulling and tugging away from the controversy. His tone became more irritable and vituperative. How does this jibe with the traditional picture we have of that soft-spoken Man of Letters who saw no evil, knew no evil, and spoke no evil?

In rapid succession Erasmus wrote letters of self-defense. In one to Jacob Banisius he called Pfefferkorn a "Pestkorn" (Latin: *Pestilentissimum granum*), and then wished that "he should have remained a total Jew or since he is circumcised, so should now his tongue and both of his hands be circumcised...." Repeating himself, as he usually did in his hateful letters when he ran out of epithets, he wrote the next day to Caesarius, "These eminent teachers of Religion utilize such a tool to undermine the peace of Christian harmony. What else could these criminal circumcised wish for, and what else their Master, the Devil, but that in this manner the harmony of the Christian People will be destroyed? ... This is Alecto, the biggest of Furies, who with Tartar trumpets sounds the signals of war, a messenger of Satan, a devils-brook, a tool of certain hypocrites, a masked protagonist for a faith, a true enemy, who as a nefarious Jew became an even more damaging Christian."[17] Then, calming down again, he managed to defend Reuchlin in calculated, but measured tones: "There is not a soul, who, as an educated and proper person, would not admit that Reuchlin experienced undignified injustice."[18] Thus he wrote to a devoted friend of Reuchlin, Count Herman von Neuenaar. But a moment later, Erasmus was off again: "Why do true Christians keep their hands off this diseased Jew (Pfefferkorn)?" Eventually he got up enough nerve and talked to Reuchlin. We notice here how Erasmus restrained himself to appear moderate, though his anti-Jewishness betrayed his intention: "Ornament of our Germany!" he addressed him in writing: "By the ever-living God, what kind of a tool do these disguised destroyers of Religion use? ... We ... despise these monsters, trust in Christ and enjoy ourselves in the pursuit of honorable studies . . . Fisher and Colet are favorable. And all learned and just men are dedicated to your cause."[19]

Jacob Hochstraten, Pfefferkorn's protector and Prior of the Dominicans in Cologne, posed as a friend of Erasmus but hated Reuchlin with a vengence. What Erasmus did not know, or ignored, was that Pfefferkorn was not alone in producing his anti-Jewish calumnies. The Dominicans had put him up to this. Erasmus now began an exchange of letters with the Prior, discussing Reuchlin, and in the course of this controversy Erasmus also became the target of Hochstraten's wrath. Erasmus wished to flatter the Prior and admonished him paternally to use the dignity of his office, his own honor, to conduct the affair in such a manner that it would reflect favorably upon his position, and also to abstain from open hatred. "You state, 'I conduct my office well' [the Inquisition]. Good and fine. However, I wish you would do it with moderation, for all to see; after all you do it in the defense of Christ, and not to evoke the impression of defending the faith as the pretext for your own ambitions and avarice or of pacifying your own private feelings of hatred. . . . You ought to discharge this investigation, not to write the verdict. But how often have you judged Reuchlin despite the fact that the trial is still going on, i.e., before a Judge, against whose judgement there is no appeal?"[20] Here is Erasmus, after using in other letters the vilest of language to berate the Jews, advising his sometime accuser to be moderate. Did he mean by that to draw fire away from himself? Or was he so insensitive that he did not see his own intolerance? In a later chapter devoted to the clinical aspects of Erasmus' make-up, we shall have ample occasion to examine the secrets of his true psyche.

Erasmus next wrote the Prior: "Your task is not to mix up Heaven and Earth and to provoke tragedies of such proportions. Oh, wouldst thou have only spent all these years of toil and trials for the propagation of the Gospel. Why waste so much brainpower to make the Jews hated? Is there anyone amongst us who does not curse this species of humans enough? If it is Christian to hate Jews, aren't we then all Christians in excess? Now, I am not saying this to protect Reuchlin, but to offer you and your colleagues advice. For he [Reuchlin] is only a friend of mine to a degree, and I do not wish to get mixed up in this affair; *that* you have equally guessed right about me...."[21] Remarks like this prompted Johan Huizinga to say: "It seems a hard thing to say that genuine loyality and fervent gratefulness were strange to Erasmus!"[22]

Max Brod, the Jewish writer, adds these perceptive observations. "It is noteworthy that Erasmus, who in his letters had taken repeatedly Reuchlin's side, ... now in a neck-breaking attempt of neutrality, which *a priori* had no change of success, committed ostentatious letters to Hochstraten, in which he tried in beauteous words to calm him down.... 'Separate the person from the issue; if this man can err, then one can condemn his error; but one must preserve his honor, his scientific striving one must hold high, etc.!...'" It was less beautiful when Erasmus appealed to the heresy-master: 'and what was so dangerous about Reuchlin's book? Was it worth so much clamor to add to the hatred against the Jews? Be content, we all hate this people!...'" And M. Brod adds: "[This proclamation of Erasmus] was a symbol of his fictitious activity. Wash my fur, but don't wet me! He could have just as well been silent. This would have been much more honest, and it would have suited better the beautiful picture of impartial moderation.... But Erasmus wanted to be a partyless man and at the same time play an active role. Thus he attempted to participate on both sides. And that does not work too well. It is more weak-kneedness [*Knieweichheit*] than genuine neutrality.... Neither Reuchlin nor Hochstraten felt through this intervention of Erasmus advantages or delighted."[23]

This is the way Erasmus treated his friends behind their backs. He shrank from being identified with this humanistic cause. He made himself liked by the Inquisitor by saying: "all good Christians hate Jews!" This was quite presumptuous on his part from the viewpoint of humanity. It was also inaccurate. There were some pro-Jewish Christian scholars and lay people to be found in the German lands. What Erasmus did not know is that during this period Jews and non-Jews in Italy had fairly decent relations, and that even the Church utilized the economic and professional services of Jews to good advantage. Thus the Humanism north of the Alps developed a Germanic character all

The Betrayal of Reuchlin and Friends   73

Luther Preaching at Wittenberg. From a painting by Cranach, the Elder.

of its own which somehow does not fit it with the claim that it ushered in western European modernity. Both Erasmus and Luther prove to modern historians that they were much closer to the Middle Ages than were their Italian counterparts. And the key to this insight is offered by Erasmus himself who resisted progress by hiding himself behind the misty facades of an already fractured Church and his own psychological inadequacies. The human tragedy is that Erasmus washed his hands of the Reuchlin-Pfefferkorn controversy, selling out a fair-minded, well-meaning, and brilliant man of his time for a pot full of inquisitional porridge, spelling out *noli me tangere:* "leave me alone, and I leave you alone." However, his duplicity came to haunt him. He knew that he was two-faced. In the heat generated by the Reformation debate Martin Luther himself called Erasmus a *Vir Duplex*, finding in his antagonist a deceptive, double dealing quality of character. Cleverly manoeuvring between Catholicism and Protestantism and avoiding decision-making, Erasmus only postured as a true Christian Renaissance man: a Man of Peace in the face of the religious internecine strife. To Pirckheimer he stated his pro-Reuchlin stand, and encouraged Reuchlin to continue the good fight in the knowledge that outstanding scholars More, Woolsey, Colet, and Fisher were behind him. The force of his anti-Semitic feelings seemed to have gotten in him the upper hand. The Jews unnerved him, and his otherwise clear mind grew agitated at the mere thought of them. Something was not quite normal in Erasmus' make-up. His attempts to caution either Reuchlin or Hochstraten to use intellectual restraint in their own controversy, sounded phony as he himself threw aside moderation at the mere mention of Jews. It is regrettable that the Jewish Erasmus scholar Guido Kisch found words of pity and extenuation for this Humanist. Speaking of moderation, Kisch had to concede, however, that "though he recommends it in his utterances about the Jews, we miss it dearly — regrettable as it is to state for an objective observer and scientific critic." [24] Kisch blamed Erasmus' attitudes on antisemitism.

Erasmus' behavior can be summarized in this way: The cause of Erasmus' ambiguity in the Reuchlin-Dominican controversy lay in his irrational hatred of the Jews. According to him they even

The Betrayal of Reuchlin and Friends 75

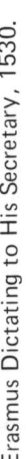

Erasmus Dictating to His Secretary, 1530.

76   *The Tragedy of Erasmus*

conspired with the Devil, who would induce fine and noble Christians to become Jews; as he put it in a letter to Carondilet, the archdeacon of Byzanz:

Where do they come from, these babbling men who more truly are camels, ... but from heretical groups? And when they are summoned before public assemblies, it is a wonder how much hellebore they seem to need.[25]

Charging them with duplicity — Pfefferkorn as a tool of Judaism — is patent nonsense. Here we have a small economically insecure people, scattered all over Europe, threatened by extinction, confiscation of property, and the loss of their Holy Books. Would such a people use a renegade to fight a losing battle by setting one Christian group against the other? It would be pure suicide. Erasmus simply did not wish to become too much identified with either the Humanists or the Reformers. He reamined a coward, yet haughty. Or did he himself feel deep in his own heart that he had no identity either? One has to give Luther credit for one thing, despite his personal brand of antisemitism he was a real fighter, and for that he was feared. He stood up for his principles and became as dogmatic as the Catholic adversary he opposed.

Just as Erasmus tried to assuage the ruffled feelings of the hierarchy for his siding with Reuchlin and for posing as a man of moderation, thus he also wished to suppress the suspicion that he was too friendly with the Catholic clerics for whom he had open contempt. He theatrically claimed wounded feelings, when he said to Thomas Woolsey: "If something goes awry, Erasmus always catches the blame. Neither Kabbala nor Talmud have ever aroused my curiosity. I met Reuchlin only once; nothing unites us but a conventional friendship as its exists between all friends in the scientific world. However, I would not be ashamed ... to come into a closer relationship with him."[26]

Erasmus was equally worried that his name might be associated with either Reuchlin's or Luther's. And he pleaded innocent: "Up till now I have not had time to study his (Luther's) books, except for a few pages.... Luther is a totally unknown person to me...."[27] This is another outright betrayal despite the fact that he reiterated the same line to the bishop of Mainz,

Cardinal Albert von Brandenberg: "I had never, neither with Reuchlin's nor with Luther's matters, anything to do. . . . I am neither a Reuchlinist nor do I belong to any humanist party . . . I am a Christian and acknowledge Christians. I do not suffer Erasmists, and I do not know any Reuchlinists. I have nothing in common with Reuchlin. Neither have I ever taken up his defense nor has he demanded one from me. . . ."[28]

This sounded rather shabby for a man who wanted to look good in the "right circles," yet had a long correspondence with the Humanists, and dreaded to let on that he was also quite comfortable in the camp of the opposition. He begged for recognition, and wrote compulsively to all the great actors of his time.[29] Max Brod put it aptly: "His striving was to maintain the dominating positions as *the* authority in all cultural questions and at the same time to elude personal danger. . . . For this reason, not out of mildness and true friendship for peace, did he wish to stay neutral. For if he had occasion to pounce upon a defenseless or tacky person as in the case of the poor Hutten — he did not do it so mildly, but with lacerating hatred — inconsiderately."[30]

Brod is referring here to the last days of the knightly fighter for true Humanism, who with his enthusiastic drive had embarrassed Erasmus as well as Luther. It was Zwingli who did not rebuff Hutten after Erasmus had ousted him fearing contagion and embarrassment. Zwingli lodged him on the Isle of Ufenau. There he died at an isolation ward. But Erasmus, the jealous meddler, was not ashamed to persuade the Council of Zurich to exile his persecuted friend. He wrote: "Hutten, if tolerated, would abuse your goodness with his lewd and audacious writings. Zurich would suffer intolerable damage because of his unbridled wantonness," and thoughtlessly Erasmus added: "he could do damage to the *evangelical* cause!" All that after Erasmus had already said goodbye to the Reformation. "The great dream of Humanism, the Brotherhood of Free Spirits, finds with this lamentable denunciation its end."[31]

However, at the very bottom of Erasmus' motivation to make Reuchlin stumble was the realization that his competitor was too busy elsewhere: Fighting for his intellectual and personal survival in the face of a persecuting Church, Reuchlin was unable to retaliate. On the other hand, Erasmus restored his own prestige by selling out an older colleague. It was Erasmus' response in also restoring his own sense of power.

In the midst of this battle Reuchlin died, at peace with himself and mourned by many. Naturally Erasmus had to mourn, too. In a humanistic pose he composed a panegyric upon his much maligned friend Reuchlin. In Erasmus' *Colloquia Familiaria* we see him standing as it were at the graveside of the only real competitor in his life: "What at one time Satan has done against the Lord through the scribes and Pharisees, that he does again now through certain Pharisees against the best men of this time. . . . Oh holy soul, be merciful to those who cultivate languages [Hebrew, Greek, and Latin] and who favored those holy tongues. But destroy the evil ones who have been affected by the poison of hell . . . ."[32]

Max Brod was repulsed by Erasmus' public weeping: "This is the same Erasmus who, as long as Reuchlin lived, pursued him with many taunts, criticized him and his language, offered cautious and half-hearted help, but then also in decisive moments mightily assisted him — a true example of a relatively cool and rickety literati-friendship. On the other hand, the modest Reuchlin was always an honest and unenvying admirer of Erasmus."[33]

The reader may still ask the relevant question: "So, why indeed did he feel the irrepressible urge to betray his friends?" We know that Erasmus did indeed identify with his Christ. And just as the Apostles betrayed Jesus in his hour of need, so did Erasmus commit the only real sin to his Father by betraying his immediate contemporary friends.

Psychologists, puzzled by man's ambivalence toward his fellow-man, have equated this attitude with moral cowardice. Thus, the Erasmian betrayal of Reuchlin and friends was one aspect of what has been called the Withdrawal Technique. As additional proof for our contention we can cite here Erasmus' unconcealed joy when the news reached him that his former friends and antagonists Zwingli and Oecolompad had died.[34] Yet to earn Christ's forgiveness, Erasmus admitted to his own wretchedness and creatureliness. At least, this made him human.

NOTES

[1] H. Graetz, *The History of the Jews* (Philadelphia, 1941), IV, pp. 422-463.

[2] *Ibid.*, p. 432 ff.

[3] Erich Hassinger conceded that the toleration of *all* religious persuasions and cult-forms and the express granting of the right to exist also extended to atheists—that this universal form of tolerance meets us in that time only within the framework of literary discussions. Erasmus offended even these generally accepted ground rules and started his own literary crusade against religious dissenters.

[4] Guillaume Budé (1467-1540), was the leading classical scholar of his time. He edited classical texts but stayed away from theological disputes, and had a greater influence in Spain and Germany than Erasmus, including more followers. In 1530 he succeeded in persuading Francis I to grant him a charter to what was to become known as the College de France, a center of modern studies (Humanist) much resented by the obscurantists of the Sorbonne.

[5] H. Graetz, p. 433.

[6] *Ibid.*, p. 434.

[7] *Ibid.*, p. 442.

[8] *Ibid.*, p. 447-448.

[9] Quoted by Max Brod, *Johannes Reuchlin und Sein Kamf* (Stuttgart, 1965), p. 239. Although not a historian, Brod had a fine gift of historical analysis and insight.

[10] *Ibid.*, p. 258.

[11] W. Welzig, *Erasmus' Letters*, Vol. II, pp. 234, 475, 471.

[12] Welzig, Vol. III, 44 ff, p. 4 ff.

[13] Pfefferkorn in the service of the Dominicans.

[14] Welzig, Vol. III, 117 ff, pp. 24-56.

[15] Letter to W. Pirckheimer in Nuremberg.

[16] Welzig, Vol. III, 122, pp. 11-15.

[17] *Ibid.*, 125f, pp. 12-42; 126ff, pp. 23-25.

[18] *Ibid.*, 128, pp. 8-10.

[19] *Ibid.*, pp. 1-14; 262, 5 ff; 291, 3 ff; 358, 20ff; 587ff, 68ff.

[20] Welzig, Vol. IV, pp. 42-51, 56, 81 ff, 108 ff, 117, 118, 139, 153.

[21] Max Brod, p. 263.

[22] Huizinga, *Erasmus and the Age of Reformation* (New York, 1957), p. 123.

[23] *Ibid.*, pp. 263-64.

[24] G. Kisch, *Erasmus' Stellung zu Juden and Judentum* (Basel, 1960), p. 20.

[25] P. S. Allen, Erasmus' *Letters* #170 (Oxford 1906-47), p. 834 ff.

[26] Welzig, Vol. III, 589, pp. 68-80.

[27] Welzig, Vol. IV, 100, pp. 34-40.

[28] *Ibid.*, 121, pp. 13-16.

[29] Similarly to Cardinal Wolsey, see P. S. Allen's footnote to p. 344.

[30] Brod, p. 31. Erasmus refused hospitality to Hutten when he knocked on his door, a dying man.

[31] Richard Friedenthal, *Luther, Sein Leben and Seine Zeit*, pp. 289 ff.
[32] Werner Welzig, *Erasmus von Rotterdam Colloquia*, p. 140-41.
[33] Brod, p. 331. One is reminded of the revolt of Carl Jung, the Swiss psychoanalyst, against Eugen Bleuler, the venerable father figure.
[34] *Erasmi Opera Omnia*, Clericus ed., Vol. III, Letters, col. 1442 B.

5
The Causes of Erasmus's Antisemitism

When Martin Luther translated the Vulgate into the vernacular German he had high hopes that the Jews too would join his Reform banner. After all, it had been the Catholic Church which had persecuted the Jews for centuries. Now, according to him, a new Church could afford to be generous, forgive the alleged crucifixion of Jesus and embrace all comers, be they pagans, heretics, or Jews. But the Jews rejected Luther's missionary zeal. As a matter of fact, at one time Jews, misunderstanding Luther's work, sent out a delegation in the hope to persuade *him* to convert to Judaism. Such was the general confusion Luther wrought with his Reform Movement. Disappointed, he heaped his scorn and contempt upon them. Luther advocated a program of destruction and deportation for the Jews, which even Kisch called "unchristian and godless, [and] which finally found its fulfillment hundreds of years later in the Third Reich."[1] Here is what Luther proclaimed from his pulpit in Eisleben, Germany, on February 15, 1546: "We must drive them out of this land when they refuse to become baptized," he declared. "For Christ commands us to be baptized and to believe in Him. But the Jews blaspheme Christ our Lord daily. Therefore, you gentlemen are not to suffer them, but drive them away. But wherever they return to us and accept Christ, so we will gladly accept them as our Brethren."[2] And in another thundering outbreak he demanded imperially: "that all their cash and jewels and silver and gold be taken away from them" and that "their synagogues or schools be set on fire, that their houses be broken up and destroyed . . . and they be put under one roof or stable like gypsies . . . in misery and captivity as they incessantly lament and complain to God about us."[3] As his contemporary Erasmus, Luther too saw the conversion of the Jews fraught with grave danger. Could they really be trusted? Perhaps the specter of the Spanish Marranos was before their minds. Luther declared, "If a Jew, not converted at heart, were to ask baptism at my hands, I would take him onto a bridge, tie a stone around his neck and hurl him into the river. For these wretches are wont to make jest of our religion."[4] This Teutonic religious barbarism expressed by the Catholic Erasmus and the Protestant Martin Luther in medieval ecclesiastical rhetoric, was to reappear in the twentieth century under the Third Reich.

Perplexed by Erasmus' anti-semitism, Kisch asked innocently: "Has he [Erasmus] had perhaps like Luther similar bad experiences with the Jews?" And he answered equally innocently: "Absolutely nothing can be detected from Erasmus' life and development." We know from Erasmus' letters that he did not meet Jews and did not even seek them out for any reason, such as dialogue, mutual learning experiences, sociability, or correspondence. Whenever he travelled, Jews were either nonexistent, as in England, where they had been barred from entry and residence, or where few in numbers, as in Germany. In the city of Basel, Switzerland, they were not allowed even to reside overnight as transients. Spain had expelled the Jews, and he knew that; he also knew that it was full of crypto-Jews (Marranos) or neo-Christians, whom he lumped together as *semi-iudei.* He was equally aware of their secret yearnings to return to their faith as soon as the circumstances permitted it; also of their presence in Italy where many of them had found refuge and means of livelihood. The only semi-iudeus he met in Italy was in the town of Pavia. In September, 1506 he was introduced to the famous Kabbalist Paulus Ricius, who later lived as a Physician at Emporer Maximilian's Court and was greatly admired for his wisdom and learning. But full-Jews he did not meet, nor did he make references to an encounter with any of them. So there must have been other motives which prompted his anti-Jewish dislikes. We

Melanchthon. From a painting by Cranach, the Elder.

have to understand his attitude within the historic context. Christianity held that it possessed the one and only truth; hence it could impose it by force. Deviationism had to be rooted out. Factionalism was not to be tolerated. Yet, both in Islam and ancient Judaism considerable freedom for internal dissent was tolerated. "Even at the height of their power, Judaism and Islam were riddled with sects and factions disputing the exact nature of the true faith. Thus their particularism encompassed a good deal of latitude. The 'truth' never became monolithic, and the notion of heresy remained rudimentary at best."[5] On the other hand, Christianity—very early in its history—produced a monolithic structure, suppressing all Christian dissent and organized campaigns against those who rejected some tenet of the Universal Church, as in the Albigensian Crusades.[6] Lastly, she invented the Inquisition, which was the very embodiment of monolithic particularism, and which gloried for centuries[7] in expediting thousands of innocents to a variety of "grotesque deaths. Such are not to be found in either ancient Judaism or Islam."[8]

Reading Erasmus' letters or his commentaries one gets the impression that he had utter contempt for the Jews; it was an outgrowth of his Christian particularism, his religious superiority complex. This contempt comes into better focus when he describes Jewish inferiority—generations after their expulsion from Spain and other countries. It is almost a truism to state that people, if they are exposed to prejudices at an early age, continue to harbor and to even develop them in later years. Since Erasmus got his training within the setting of a church school, we may assume that his heart was prejudiced against the Jews very early in his life. When he left the Brethren, Erasmus became rootless. He ran from one end of western Europe to the other, he was the most widely travelled humanist of his time. And he ran for reasons which will be explored. It is enough to suggest at this time that he hated himself for being a man without a home, a rootless wanderer. Psychologically speaking, a horrible image presented itself before his mental eye: He saw the Jews, a rootless people, migrating or driven from one part of Europe to the other. Whether he liked the resemblance or not, he identified with them. They were the Eternal Wanderers, and he was likewise an eternal

Luther. From a painting by Cranach, the Elder.

intellectual vagrant. And just as he felt driven and did not permit himself to ever rest, so did he wish to disperse Jews, and condemn them to eternal restlessness. How horrible it must have been for Erasmus to live with himself in his own psychological agony. Had he become a real Humanist, enlightened like Melanchthon or Reuchlin, perhaps even taken the step toward a more liberal approach to Christianity by way of the Reformation, things may have become different. As A. G. Dickens has pointed out: "Anti-Semitism was one of the many unchristian aspects of Medieval Christian society."[9] Erasmus' prejudice against Jews was not just another case of xenophobia. They were a real threat to him and they sounded in him a psychological alarm bell. He had two choices: either to flee from them or to fight them. Erasmus' paradoxical character chose both alternatives: he became the restless traveller, uneasy with himself, wherever he went; and he fought them with his pen. This attitude we can safely call his belligerence. But beyond that, from the analytical point of view, we can pose this problem: Was Erasmus of such inner violence and turmoil that he had to destroy or devour this people (the Jews) for fear that he might die? In the words of Benjamin B. Wolman: "Those who fear, hate; and those who hate, fear." And he concludes: "According to the Thánatos [death] Theory, aggression is merely an outwardly directed self-destructive instinct of death."[10] We have always to remember the Erasmus was and remained a faithful son of the orthodox medieval Catholic Church, and that his occasional flirtations with the Reformers cannot stamp him a fellow-traveller or secret member of the New Church. Since he was committed to the old-time religion, and since he hated controversy caused by new commitments, Erasmus was safe.[11]

Furthermore, as we have indicated before, Erasmus was a dedicated though "selective" Old Testament scholar. He was familiar with the minutiae of Jewish legislation, practices and beliefs, ceremonial and dietary laws, feasts and fasts, habits and times of religious assembly. All of these represented in his medieval mind that which his Master, Jesus, had rejected and which he called Pharisaism. To Erasmus, the Jews of his time were German Pharisees, and he could hate them, because Jesus too had unkind words to say about them. What Erasmus objected to, and which found him in the same camp with Martin Luther, was the Jewish preoccupation with the observance of the Mitzvoth, the laws and rules of Jewish life. But the starting point for this anti-Pharisaic posture is Erasmus' contempt, again resembling Luther's feeling, for the over-emphasis on doing "good deeds" within the confines of the Catholic Church. That Erasmus misunderstood the Jewish Theology of observing Mitzvoth is clear, just as Jesus' reprimand of Pharisaic theology, was not a rejection of the Pharisees themselves to whom be belonged, but with whom he differed drastically and emotionally. Besides, the situation there, fifteen hundred years prior to Erasmus, was far different from the times of the Reformation squabble. Had Erasmus looked at Jesus as a Reformer of Judaism, our guess is that as a loyal Catholic, Erasmus would have rejected him just as vehemently as he rejected Luther's reformism. Erasmus did not believe in the Jewish Salvation theory, just as he abhorred Catholic Christian stressing of good works as a means toward Salvation.[12] As a good Catholic he was bothered by the survival of Old Testament ritual and moral teaching in the Church. And Christian clerics did not break away decisively enough from the lessons and spirit of the Old Testament. They were guilty of trying to give both Testaments, the old and the new, equal time. To him this was tantamount to treason. Jews and Christians were not to learn from each other. This was their common guilt.

Erasmus expressed his views clearly to Paul Volz, taking Franciscans and Benedictines equally to task. He worte: "May this *not* to be true for the majority of them. I do not scoff that some of them eat fish, others vegetables and herbs, while others again eat eggs. However, I do have second thoughts that they might be in grave error, who are convinced with Jewish conviction to be justified and because of such ridiculousness, which were invented by poor people [the Jews], regard themselves as better than others; whilst they see nothing wrong to attack the reputation of a foreigner [Erasmus] with outright lies."[13] That Jews observed "senseless rituals" was their business, though contemptible. However, Christians should know better. And if they did not, then this was "iudaizare," as he termed it, Jew-loving! The other stumbling block for Erasmus was this: while the Jews did not produce a visible sectarianism or a fracturing of their unity, clinging to their Faith despite persecution, contempt and untold suffering—of which he was surely aware—the Christian Religion offered the spectacle of diffusion of strength, of a deep religious split. The Jews may be a people brought low by God for their blindness, for not accepting the Savior, but the Christian Church was in the midst of a self-destructing death throe which he, the Humanist, could neither prevent nor cure.[14]

In all fairness, Erasmus did respect the Old Testament but with this qualification: it was good for its moral stories, it taught character and, in typical Humanistic fashion, he held the importance of Hebrew studies a must; at least for theologians and Humanists; it certainly was not good for the masses. But at the same time, there was no question in his mind that the New Testament held the sole truth; that it had superceded the Old; that it was the exclusive source of salvation. Here we can witness one of Erasmus' many paradoxical attitudes. He realized that Hebrew should be taught by Christian scholars, that it ranked with Greek and Latin as the third most important language to be studied and even revered. Yet, saying all this, he also recognized the great danger of this pursuit to a missionizing Christian Faith. As he said in one of his letters: "How much arduous labor was it for Paul to emancipate Christ from Judaism. I have the feeling that some will secretely relapse, and will put things into motion, which will have nothing to do with the knowledge of Christ, but will only throw sand into the eyes of people. All studies ought to be solely dedicated to Christ."[15] This, one must admit, is a rather narrow interpretation of his Faith. But against those who hold that this stand of Erasmus was typically Humanist, the modern interpreter must come to the conclusion that it represented the last gasp of Medievalism.

There is little in the mere fact of being a Christian Humanist, a Renaissance man, an exponent of Reformation, to guarantee enlightenment and freedom from barbarism. Erasmus and his contemporaries who shared in the movements called Humanism, Renaissance, and Reformation were not wholly transformed; they went on being human, following their own lights, unable to

Causes of Erasmus' Anti-Semitism 89

Pope Paul IV (1555-1559), the Founder of the Ghetto. From a contemporary engraving.

foretell the future. They went on acting according to their historical and psychic pasts, however modern they may sometimes seem to be, and however attractive may be the vague labels put on them by our contemporaries. Luther, Reuchlin, Erasmus, and others are carelessly grouped by historians; they place these men in the Humanist, or the Reformation, or the Renaissance camp, or in two or three camps, and even call them transitional Modernists. This is confusing. One may say that these men lived at the "end of a dark tunnel" and perhaps pushed Medievalism over the cliff and embarked consciously or unconsciously, on a more enlightened road without knowing where this road might lead to. Yet, as children of the medieval times they were always pulled back to it as a growing child has a hankering to return to the bosom of its mother. To force the great personages of a given period into a historic straight-jacket is an idle intellectual exercise. Besides it is inaccurate. Christians were an unchallenged majority in Western Europe in the sixteenth century. Jews and Moslems were not invited to play an immediate role in the Humanist Renaissance. They had other problems: to escape persecution and to survive as naked human beings; or, as in the case of the Moors and Turks, to fight for geo-political influence in eastern Europe and the Mediterranean.

The western European Jews either lived in ghettos, or where the eternally wandering merchandizers and "usurers," or were pushed around by their contemporaries, who were always in the majority. This pertains also in the intellectual area. Jewish sages, rabbis, or commentators were concerned with their own people in terms of physical and spiritual survival. And if some Jews played a part in what is called Humanism (as in Italy), then it was usually at the expense of their own Jewishness. Jewish Humanism was assimiliationist in nature and was rejected by Torah-true Jews as well as by the exponents of Humanism.

We witness in Renaissance Humanism a shifting from the theological to the secular, without becoming either anti-Christian or anti-religious. It was the thirst for self-expression, caused by economic factors, which established for the first time in western Christendom priorities for a meaningful life. M. Jacques Maritain summed up this thought most clearly when he stated: "The radiating dissolution of the Middle Ages and its consecrated forms represents (at the same time) the birth of a secular civilization, one that is indeed not wholly secular, but which as it advances, servers itself more and more from Incarnation." [16]

A little more than one hundred years had to go by until Baruch Benedict Spinoza had overcome medieval Humanism and Reformation Christianity by epitomizing the best of truly new thinking when he said: "I have made a ceaseless effort not to ridicule, not to bewail and not to scorn human actions, but to understand them." None of these words could have been said or thought by Erasmus or would be applicable in an honest evaluation of The Light of Humanism.[17] This clarion call for a truly moral, religious and ethical Christian Weltanschauung was beyond the reach of this tragic man, Erasmus.

But then, we have to understand that Spinoza wrote down these words because he was a Jew with parents who had cared for him by giving their son a home, an education, and love. Erasmus experienced nothing of this kind. The Christ became his Father-substitute and surrogate who would suffer no unchristian deviationism.

NOTES

[1] Kisch, G. in *Erasmus' Stelling zu Juden und Judentum*, p. 9 ff.
[2] Quoted from Luther's *Werke, Erlangen Edition*, Vol. 65, pp. 186-89.
[3] Quoted in William L. Shirer *The Rise and Fall of The Third Reich* (New York, 1960), p. 236.
[4] Luther's *Table Talk* #275.
[5] Charles Y. Glock and Rodney Stark, *Christian Beliefs and Antisemitism* (New York, 1966), p. 32 f.
[6] During the campaign against the Albigensians, the papal legate reported to Pope Innocent III "that our men, sparing neither rank nor sex nor age, slew about 20,000 souls with the edge of the sword; and, making a huge slaughter, pillaged and burned the whole city, by reason of God's wrath wondrously kindled against it." When later asked about the danger that some Christians might also be slain in these wholesale annihilations of cities, the legate is reported to have advised, "Slay all, the Lord will know his own." Quotations from H. C. Lea, *A History of the Inquisition in Spain* (New York, 1906-1967), Vol. I, pp. 215, 135.
[7] The Inquisition was officially terminated only in the first quarter of the nineteenth century.
[8] Glock and Stark, pp. 33-35.
[9] A. G. Dickens: *Martin Luther and The Reformation* (New York, 1967), p. 139.
[10] *The Psychoanalytic Interpretation of History*, in "Sense and Nonsense in History" (New York, 1971), p. 97 ff.
[11] George Gebhardt, *Die Stellung des Erasmus zur Roemischen Kirche* (Marburg, 1966), pp. 1-412.
[12] Werner Welzig: *Erasmus Colloquia Familiaria*, Vol. VII (Darmstadt, 1967), p. 64 ff. Also Elsbeth Gutmann: *Die Colloquia Familiaria* (Basel 1968), p. 133. And Alfred Hartman, *Das Lob der Torheit* (Basel, 1943), p. 90.
[13] W. Welzig, *Epistola a Paulum Volzium* (Darmstadt, 1968), pp. 40-41.
[14] Welzig,*Erasmus Letters*, Vol. VI, 489, 240-245.
[15] Welzig, *Letters*, Vol. II, 491 ff, pp. 147-154.
[16] *True Humanism* (1939), p. 8.
[17] Guido Kisch

6
Crazy-Quilt Theology and Ethics

Unlike Johan Reuchlin who learned to appreciate ancient Hebrew culture and developed a fondness for Judaism, Erasmus remained aloof from this integral part of antiquity and learning. He had reasons for his alienation from that "barbaric" culture. As J. W. Aldridge pointed out,

> The ancient civilizations of Egypt, Babylonia, and Syria, or for that matter, Israel, were never considered as important to Erasmus as were the civilizations of Rome and Greece. The cause for it lay in the fact that these more ancient periods were not open to him as were the classical periods. Therefore, when Erasmus says that he wishes an age built on the best of antiquity, he envisions a return to the culture of Rome and Greece rather than a return to the earlier golden age of the Middle East.

> Our age is so different from Erasmus' time that it is difficult to envision the thinking of the Middle Ages on the point in question. The Middle Age man did not have the advantage of the manuscripts, art, and archeological discoveries that we have available today. To say that the Middle Age knowledge of these ancient periods was clouded by darkness is an understatement, for it was also clouded by myths and superstitions, thereby making the few ascertainable facts of doubtful value. The oriental mind and its ideas were alien to the Middle Ages and the gifts to the world little understood and little utilized. Erasmus himself was under the same impressions as his age, and thereby did not understand the real life and culture of these ancient people. To him the people of the old Testament are little more than barbarians.[1]

This statement in form of a apologia sounds too simple to be convincing. What is true is that Romanism was western oriented, and that the western Christian had little in common with the eastern orthodox. However, Erasmus' entire *Philosophia Christi* was based on thorough study and subsequent hateful denigration of Old Testament literature. Three hundred years earlier St. Thomas, with his neo-Aristotelian posture, was more of a "Humanist"—paradoxically as it may sound—than Erasmus who had blinders when it came to a dispassionate discussion of Judaism. Furthermore, Aldridge is contradictory in what he had to say later on: "His [Erasmus'] was a high regard for the Old Testament both as a background of Christianity and as a source book of Christianity, but he was limited in his ability to comprehend its full meaning and significance."[2] Erasmus was not ashamed to choose those portions of the Old Testament which served his prejudiced mind, and to reject those that were "barbaric." He made that clear in his letter to John Caesarius: "I had rather that the Old Testament should be altogether abolished, than that the peace of Christendom be destroyed for the sake of all the books of the Jews."[3] This is the overriding issue — not that the culture of the Jews was oriental! Granted, not all of the original ancient sources were available to Erasmus, but his contemporaries, such as Reuchlin and Pico, knew and tried to understand Old Testament literature, even the Talmud and the Kabbala. What Erasmus did not see was that the humanist era had been fructuated by the Jews and their scholarship which became so decisive during the Reformation controversy. As B. Lazare expressed it: "During these years which ushered in the Reformation the Jew turned educator, and taught the scholars Hebrew; he initiated them into the mysteries of the kabbala after having opened to them the doors of Arabic philosophy. Against Catholicism he equipped them with the formidable exegesis which the rabbis had cultivated and built up during centuries: the exegesis which Protestantism, and later on rationalism, would make good use of. By a singular chance the Jews, who had consciously or unconsciously supplied humanism with weapons, had also given it the pretext for its first serious battle. The contest for or against the Talmud was the forerunner of the disputes over the Eucharist."[4]

Erasmus did not *wish* to know all that was available in the university libraries (Louvain, for instance), or in monasteries. His attitude reveals once more the studied ambiguity: he was more conversant with Jewish culture than he let on in his *Theology.* Aldridge's apologia continues: "Erasmus is more interested in his ideals than in the Old Testament itself. . . . The superstition, shadows, and lack of culture [!] in the Old Testament make it pre-Christian in meaning. The ancient superstition which sometimes flows through the passages and stories of the Old Testament covers the truth of the message. This, together with the cruelty and barbaric ways of the peoples represented, presented to Erasmus a lack of culture that was directly opposed to his personal principles of gentleness, simplicity, and the like. As a person who saw the philosophia Christi as the way to combat the above-mentioned things that were so abominable to him, it is no wonder that he was never able to give the Old Testament a place equal to the New Testament." This is an academic distortion. It only proves that Erasmus, by his own admission, did not wish to understand the Jews in time and place. Craig R. Thompson in his forword to W. H. Woodward's Desiderius Erasmus, *Concerning the Aim and Method of Education* had a clearer conception: "Erasmus [thus again] reveals his lack of concern for the elements of [Jewish] national life, and his ignorance of the true basis of national [Jewish] culture."[5] Indeed, the Old Testament writers did not compose the Bible as a selective source book for moralizing pietists; they were not ashamed to record both the good and the bad of the peoples that figured in Hebrew Antiquity over three thousand years ago. The Old Testament is the collective record of Semitic and other peoples. It is the mirror of an age that saw the Hebrews grow from desert beduins into the People of God under Law, marching from slavery to freedom, from pagan innocence to the lofty heights of a morality that is binding for all times and for the western world. To say that Erasmus did not know that, is misleading.

Erasmus' contemporaries, such as Reuchlin, Pico della Mirandola, Melanchton, Postell and many unknown others, wrestled with their faith, to make it more meaningful for themselves, especially in view of the intra-Christian debacle of a church-busting Reformation. The Jews loved their God and they had remained His people by doing His commandments and listening to His word. To Erasmus, God as Father was remote. It was his Christ, his new fatherhead, that he tried, in an act of desperation, to recapture and to know. But he ended up talking and writing about Him, fighting for Him in the face of real and imaginary enemies. And in the process he himself did not even come to worship Him! This is the tragic feeling one gets from reading his vast correspondence or treatises. It is sad to see this often "careless" philologist[6] use every trick of the trade,[7] irony, wit, and sarcasm to ingratiate himself with his adopted real father, Christ, and to curry favors and prestige with his peers on the left and on the right.

Erasmus became in his time a most embattled and controversial man, converting his erstwhile friends into his bitterest enemies. He became the undoer of his own genius. The Belgian historian Henri Pirenne in an appraisal of the Humanist's posture toward the Church expressed his views this way: "The intellectual History of Europe was merely a chapter in the History of the Church (since Pope Gregory in 604) with Latin as her international language in which God spoke to man and vice versa! And Erasmus in the absence of a truly religious Pope and Church-leaders postured as her self-appointed Secretary of State.... He became the Prop-maker for Church Dogmas."[8]

In the light of these poignant observations, we can now proceed to summarize Erasmus' "theological" views of Judaism. The Jews were reprehensible to Erasmus (an observing Catholic) because they underscored the doing of the Law, and they got wrapped up in good works. "They twisted the Law," and "when their absurd teachings were in conflict with something from Scripture, they would twist Scripture to fit their own peculiar interpretation." In a letter to Servetus in 1514 he wrote: "I know not what image of Christ you will find, unless you can so regard some cold Jewish ordinances...." And again: "they twist the Law to refer not to Christ but to some other Messiah, for whom they have unfruitfully waited for so many centuries."[9] Beyond that, "The Jews, at first, held tenaciously to that to which they were accustomed (the Law), much like a child used to sucking at the breast, even when it has grown robust, will cry for the breast and slight more solid food [*i.e.* the Christian dogma]. But they were forced, as it were, from those symbols, shadows and temporary comforts." So, what are their Laws? Erasmus answered: "Superstitions" and "outward observances" such as "circumcision, which the Jews endeavored to thrust upon the Gentiles" or "divorces which can be obtained on frivolous grounds," or being forbidden "to study the Book of Genesis before the thirtieth birthday."[10] Naturally, Erasmus held that "The Jews crucified the Lord with the purpose of removing him completely. This wicked plan God turned to the honor of his son, and to the welfare of the whole world."[11] After the death of Jesus the Jews were broken off. And Paul, Erasmus believed, told us why: "Paul [the Jew!] served less in refuting the freedom of the will, than in dampening the arrogance of the Jews, who believed that the Gospel's grace was to be theirs alone by virtue of their descent from Abraham."

In other words and in the phraseology of Erasmus: Paul "aims at rebuffing the godlessly grumbling Jews, who have been rejected from the grace of the Gospels." And he summed up his *Discourse on Free Will:* "No other wisdom may be taught among Christians than that which is 'hidden in a mystery,' and this belongs only to the 'perfect'—and not to the sons of a Judaizing, legal-minded generation, who, without faith, boast of their works."[12]

In all justice to Erasmus, we must admit that he had on occasion something good to say about the Jews: In the lines on *Cicero*, Erasmus reminded us that it was commonly held that before Christ came, a confused faith concerning divine matters— sufficed for the salvation of good Hebrews. They did not have explicit faith in Christ; implicit faith was enough. So there was a hope even for them. The door for salvation of the Jew was kept slightly ajar. However, whether Erasmus was truly comfortable with this random thought, is anybody's guess.[13] At least, he held an olive branch to the "righteous pagans" and their chances after death. In the words of C. R. Thompson: "It is not difficult, therefore, to understand why Erasmus says in his *Encomium* of Cicero that the Virtuous pagans' chances after death were like those of the ancient Hebrews who, before Christ came, lived under and kept the Mosaic law. We may believe that those pagans, like those Hebrews, were saved; at the very least we have no grounds for assuming they were not saved."

It does not behoove us at the end of this century in which liberal Christian theologians have convincingly refuted Erasmus' type of medieval theology, to restate the "Jewish Position." What interests us in this context, even ignoring Erasmus' intemperate language, is this: Erasmus' *real* targets where the officials and officiating clergy of the Catholic Church on the one hand[14] and Monasticism on the other. The former were depicted as slothful, gluttonous and lewd, focusing on the observance of rituals, while the latter was governed by narrow asceticism, laid down by the Church, and totally nonproductive. This Erasmian impatience aimed at undermining the medieval tradition, but was turned by Martin Luther into a New Theology. Erasmus never achieved that kind of fame. His attacks were nothing else but noisy rhetoric, essentially pagan, as Bronowski has pointed out.[15] To compound matters, Erasmus tendentiously used the Jews as the instrument with which to whip Church, Monasticism, and ultimately in a turn-about: the Jewish People! He laid himself, therefore, wide open to the accusation of anti-intellectualism though he vacillated between the acrimonious tradition of yesteryear and the new mood of Humanism of his time.[16]

Von Koerber, who more or less identified Erasmus' Humanism with the Latin *humanitas*, also does not sound convincing. To him his "*humanitas* embraces freedom, namely the inner freedom in the Christian sense, such as human dignity."[17] This sounds beautiful, yet it lacks convincing flavor as one looks at the total man Erasmus, who lacked inner freedom, though he talked about it, and who did not achieve full human dignity.

Conversely, Erasmus fought unrealistically for a man's so-called dual citizenship, secular and religious, in this *Res Publica Christiana*, so that religion became a matter of state ("they had almost a Department of Religious Affairs"). It was utopian. "Erasmus' effort to civilize and to pacify western Europe through a fusion of pagan and Christian values was smashed by the Protestant Reformation."[18]

Erasmus sensed his failure; and the failure of his proposed Commonwealth might explain his later hatred of Luther as he had

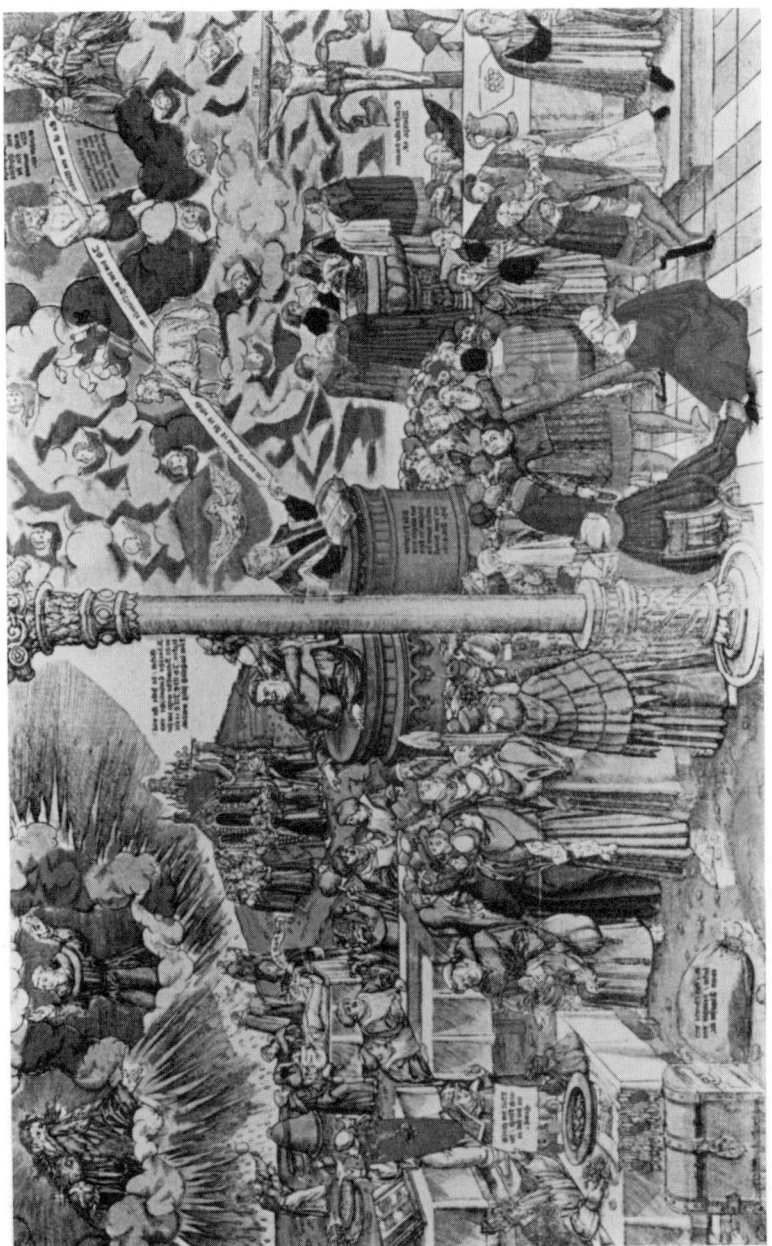

Luther's Service Attended by Christ, the Pope, and the Elector. From a painting by Cranach, the Elder.

to surrender his leadership to a bigger man. William Harrison Woodward offers us another, equally lucid explanation for the Erasmian reaction to Luther's work: "But it is true to say that the only region in which he had any thought-out system to offer for guidance of a practical world was the region of Latin scholarship and of education. And Erasmus knew it. His shrinking from partisan declarations was but the recognition of the fact that both in theological dialect and in ecclesiastico-political fighting the two dominant sides of the Lutheran struggle, he was no expert, and had neither the gifts nor inclinations to become one."[19] "Years will come," said Huizinga, "in which his enormous correspondence is little more than one protracted self-defense."[20] On the other side of the spectrum is the French historian Augustine Renaudet. He agrees with this writer, who maintains that Erasmus was in some form a Humanist, certainly in the area of education and classical philology, and only then a "pious" Christian. Likewise Adolph Harnack, looking for a renewal of Paulinism, writes, that Erasmus was—note his careful phrasing—"the hero of an era of adcendancy." He too was avoiding the term Christian Humanism.[21] It has not escaped the critics that Erasmus, despite his Brethren of the Common Life upbringing, had turned against the mystical elements of his own Church, the dogmatic and sacramental. He replaced them with a moral—if not impatiently intolerant—dogmatism of his own. Perhaps this is the true reason why he only flirted with Protestantism in the beginning. The other may be attributed to his almost innate revulsion against having a deep commitment to any cause but his own. Or as Renaudet phrased it: his position "was due to his timidity and temperament than to deep convictions." What is so amazing is that Erasmus, despite his schooling with the Brethren, showed "a lack of understanding of the mystical basis of monasticism that led him to judge it as a useless way of life, and . . . that he neither had the spirit nor the temperament of an heresiarch."[22] Small wonder then, that he was also unable to understand Judaism and its concept of holiness which manifests itself in the free exercise of the Mitzvoth, the commandments. Erasmus lacked the in-depth view of all religion. What is left was a cold Socratic approach and a surrender to the world of ideas which could not be grafted upon the mysterium of

Peasant Celebrant. Priest Plows by Joseph Grunbeck, 1508, Nuremberg.

the Godhead and his ever continuing revelation to all mankind. If, as Erasmus believed, piety alone, as a pedogogical exercise, could bring man closer to the Christ, then he was not saying much. Because piety in itself is wholly negative. It is other-worldly. Only piety combined with the "to do" makes man truly a religious being. A Christian becomes a Christian not merely by meditation about his Savior or in asceticism, but by also performing his teachings. Otherwise he winds up a misdirected romantic, landing in the never-never land of ideas, and the state of unhappy withdrawal so typical of Erasmus, the man without lasting friends. The very *Res Publica Christiana* Erasmus dreamed about looks now more and more like a Worldwide Oratory, composed of ecstatic, believing, meditating Jesus-freaks who find themselves in an almost unreal paradiso, knowing neither a *unio mystica* nor a *communio cum deo*,[23] doing nothing, but escaping from responsibility, surrendering to a Society of No-Progress and Non-Culture. It was essentially the philosophy of the Essenes at Qumran that Erasmus favored — not knowing then what we know today: that they too disappeared from history because of their "unreal" view of God and a life-giving Messiah. . . .[24]

The Erasmian Ethic shows the humanist's paradox: it is a mixture of traditional Catholic but also neo-Protestant currents. If one adds to this Erasmus' preoccupation with the ancients, we come up with an interesting quilt pattern which—though unconsciously felt—made him quite uncomfortable. Erasmus believed, of course, what the medieval Church had sanctioned right along: that man was unfree as far as life, liberty, and the pursuit of happiness were concerned; that man had fallen "from Grace"; that his flesh was weak and put him in constant trouble with his conscience—and beyond that with society. Man was faced by unknown antagonists which made him stumble and keep him in sin. This is a rather negative approach to life because it puts man in bondage unless and until he is saved. He remains here on earth the captive of terrifying forces which test or sap his strength and yet keep him weak and suffering, unable to escape psychological hurts and agony.

Thus, medieval man remained passive and stoic—contemptuous of this world and submitting to the fates. In such a world man cannot achieve what we may call peace of mind and soul. The Church had deprived man of initiative and resolution. He became a slave; he remained unfree to develop social values within his society, or strength to develop a sense of obligation toward others. The latter attitude is decisive, at least in our case. For Erasmus fits into this theological-ethical framework. It explains his inability to cope with internal and external forces, his misanthropic attitude toward friends and colleagues, his unresolve in the face of psychic difficulties, but equally important, his curious and probing attitude toward the Reformation. Erasmus was born at a stressful time,[25] when new but risky possibilities of social, religious, and economic change offered themselves. Erasmus wanted change without risk.

The other issue was this: Erasmus could not deal with his "guilt" simply because the Church did not offer any clear-cut guidelines to cope with personal guilt or sin. One has to ask: Was the medieval Church qualified to relieve man's pressures that sapped man's inner strength? I do not think so. To do this, she needed more sophistication and intellectual experience. Hers was an experience with Faith and Works, but not to serve the psychic or social needs of her children. The Church had not discovered as yet that man is also a *social* creature with responses and responsibilities, as O. Hobart Mowrer has pointed out in *Psychiatry and Religion:* "we are coming to perceive man as pre-eminently a social creature, whose greatest and most devastating anguish is experienced not in physical pain or biological deprivation but when he feels alienated, disgraced, guilty and debased as a person." [26]

Erasmus dreamt about a united Christianity and its purposeful return to its ancient beginnings, to the Paradiso, reigned over by the Christ in Socratic purity and benevolence. To him this life of bliss promised normalcy, but to us moderns it was a rather unheroic existence. It was unreal and nonprogressive. It stood still in time and forestalled history.

NOTES

[1] J. W. Aldridge, *The Hermeneutic of Erasmus* (Winterthur, 1966), p. 41.
[2] *Ibid.*, p. 46.
[3] J. H. Allen, *Hebrew Men and Times* (Boston, 1883), Letter #701.
[4] *Antisemitism* (New York, 1903).
[5] J. W. Aldridge, pp. 48, 64.
[6] Cornelius Reedijk, *What Is Typically Dutch in Erasmus?* (New York, 1959), p. 37. "He cannot always be absolved from the charge of carelessness...."
[7] His friend Ammonius called it the "hilaritas Erasmi."
[8] Henri Pirenne, *Histoire economique et sociale du Moyen age* (Paris, 1969).
[9] John P. Dolan, *The Essential Erasmus*, "On Mending the Peace of the Church" (Toronto, 1967), pp. 207-284.
[10] W. Welzig, Commentary to Erasmus' *Hyeraspistes II*, Vol. IV, p. 359.
[11] Ernest F. Winter, *Erasmus and Luther*, "Discourse on Free Will" (Vienna, 1969), p. 50.
[12] *Ibid.*, pp. 45, 56, 114.
[13] Craig R. Thompson, Commentary on *Inquisitio De Fide* (Chicago, 1965), pp. 117-119.
[14] See Erasmus' *Julius Exclusus*, translated by Paul Pascal (Bloomington/London, 1950), p. 50.
[15] Jacob Bronowski, *Man Out of Season* (St. Marian, Ohio, 1962), p. 89 ff.
[16] Albert Salomon, *Democracy and Religion in the Work of Erasmus* (New York, 1950), p. 229.
[17] Von Koerber: *Rechtliche Grundfragen der res-publica Christiana*, IV, p. 87.
[18] R. Dunn, *The Age of Religious Wars* (New York, 1970), p. 209.
[19] D. *Erasmus concerning the Aim and Method of Education* (New York, 1956), p. 25.
[20] J. Huizinga, *Erasmus and The Age of Reformation* (New York, 1957), p. 122.
[21] Hanns Rueckert, *The Reformation—Medieval or Modern* (Tuebingen, 1965), p. 5.
[22] August Renaudet, *Erasme, sa Pensee Religieuse et son Action, d'apres son Correspondance* (Geneva, 1970), pp. 13-14, 34.
[23] A mystical oneness or communion with God.
[24] Spermatikos.
[25] It is interesting to see how this new Protestant ethic, combined with Greek stoicism, is essentially also the Ethic of Sigmund Freud, as Richard LaPiere has pointed out in his article, *The Freudian Ethic* (Liege, 1964), p. 306.
[26] O. Hobart Mowrer, *Psychology and Religion* (Princeton, 1964), pp. 323-324.

7

The Reluctant Hebraist

The scientific study of the Hebrew language was not the product of the Reformation Age. It was the product of a tradition—Judaism. Its teachers and commentators nourished it through the centuries and influenced the Christian world. Not even the almost ecstatic Christian Reform could check its influence. Yet, at the end of the Middle Ages the actual knowledge of the Hebrew language—reaching into the beginning of the sixteenth century of western Europe—had not found much acclaim in the schools of higher learning. At first, Humanism, with its declared ideal to revive the classics, approached Hebrew with a kind of mental reservation and apprehension. This was quite natural. After all, there were no Christian Hebrew scholars around, just as there were few experts in Greek. To take the daring step of inviting Jewish teachers to instruct Christian Humanists was unthinkable. The early humanist, R. Agricola (1467-1535), found Hebrew an "unusual and distressing burden." He wrote: "Look at my blunders, I beg you—or my stupidity—I have decided to learn Hebrew just so that my too-little time and labor in these very few Greek matters may be lost to me. . . . Those matters add to this study of Hebrew, which appears to me new and full of bother, so that I seem to myself to be struggling with Antacus."[1]

The same goes for the so-called Tuebingen Theologians, among them Conrad Pellican, Ulrich Zwingli's friend. But the enthusiastic Humanist slogan "Back to the Sources!", meant for many including Hebrew as a vital matter for consideration. Thus it became rather fashionable to dabble at first in Hebrew, with Greek and Latin, and to amass large libraries before one could even read, write, or translate them, as in the case of Johann of Dalburt, the Bishop of Worms. It was not until Reuchlin that this language became part and parcel of Humanistic exploration, cultivation, and intense study. He himself became the first truly competent Hebrew scholar in the Germanic Lands.

Reuchlin approached the mass of Hebrew Literature with the earnestness of a scientific modernist, while Erasmus faced up to it like a still-immature man who feels attracted and at the same time repelled at the sight of a beautiful woman with a past. One recalls his famous statement written in a letter to Albrecht of Brandenburg: "Kabbala and Talmud, whatever they may be, have never smiled upon me." Envious as he was of Reuchlin's genius and reputation, and also knowing that the New Trend, this Humanist Mood, demanded the inclusion of Hebrew amongst the classical languages, Erasmus sooner or later had to face up to it himself. However, in the meanwhile he lashed out at Reuchlin, his friend: "He studies this language from German and Italian Jews, whom he approaches without contempt, yes, to whom he offers grateful veneration as his Masters. He buys in Italy Hebrew and Chaldeic (*i.e.* Aramaic) books, registers conscientiously place and time of the first meeting by looking upon his treasures. He teaches and writes in private and then to the streaming [hordes of his] disciples in public."[2] He was referring to Reuchlin's small volume on the Hebrew language,[3] which by modern standards could only be called rudimentary. But it was a beginning.

Even in Spain, particularly at the Universities of Alcalá and Valladolid Hebrew had made great inroads, which Erasmus, of course, regretted. Since Holland was under the dominance of Spain, he did not have much liking for the Spaniards. He despised them for their overbearing manners and obtrusiveness which he attributed to their Jewish inbreeding. J. Beumer, S. J., contended that Erasmus' antipathy toward the Spaniards was not necessarily the result of their "miscegenation" with the Marranos, but because he felt inferior toward his fellow Hebrew scholars because they had an edge over him: they were ex-Jews and hence better prepared in the Biblical Scriptures than he. So it was envy that stimulated his antisemitism. "The deeper reason," wrote Beumer, "for his aversion remains unclear. Perhaps Erasmus with his antisemitism, which was not suited to his character at all, resisted the exegetics (commentators) of Alcala, who, because of their Jewish origin were vastly superior in the knowledge of the Hebrew language."

Erasmus admitted two years before Reuchlin's short manual was published that he too had become casually involved with that language. In a letter to Colet he wrote: "I have also started to study the Hebrew Language, but was scared away because of its strangeness. I gave it up."[4] As a contrast the reader may recall Reuchlin's words that Hebrew is the holy language in which God confers directly with man. Eleven years later Erasmus would write to his friend Johannes Reuchlin: "I do not pretend to be a Hebraist, after all I have tasted it only very superficially."[5] It is interesting to ask why he was so reluctant to study Hebrew, or why he pleaded old age, or why he made so light of it? It is possible that Erasmus confused Hebrew with Yiddish, a *lingua franca* based upon a High German dialect. He could speak German only poorly, and ignorance might well have caused this remark: "Hebrew is little known, and, even by the Jews, spoken in a corrupt way."[6] With such a confusion in mind, he could the more easily have transferred his dislike of Jews to a language—Hebrew— which they allegedly did not even speak well.

The French Renaissance King, Francis I, made his greatest contribution when he founded and sponsored the Trilingual college which specialized in the teaching of Greek, Latin, and Hebrew as preliminary to the study of the Classics. The magisters of the Sorbonne fulminated against this cultivation of humanistic learning and called it "a nursery for heretics." The School flourished under Busleiden, added gradually professorial chairs and then expanded its curriculum to include the sciences. Francis' elaborately collected manuscripts from Syria, Egypt, and Constantinople were the backbone of this institution.

By 1517 the Collegium Trilingue was the most famous among the classical European institutions of Higher Learning, founded by Hieronymous Busleiden,[7] in the Belgian city of Loewen (in the

Brabant). It was there that Erasmus got a glimpse at Greek and Latin studies but also of the Hebraica Veritas, where to search for the true meaning of the Old Testamental text was the primary goal of all learning. It was in the Spring of the following year that Erasmus asked his friend Oecolompad to help him again with Hebrew under the pretext that he intended to be in Basel by May of 1518 to take care of his new edition of the New Testament. In the same year his friend Bersilius introduced him to a Hebrew teacher, Johannes Vellarius. On the occasion of the second edition of his *New Testament*, he again mentioned Hebrew in the Introduction: "Although I have reached already my fifty-third year, I shall, if that is possible, return to the Hebrew language, of which I have partaken only superficially." [8]

While he recognized the need for Humanists to pursue the Hebrew tongue, he had second thoughts. His medieval theological prejudices got the upper hand over humanist, philosophic considerations. In a frank letter to his friend Fabricius Capito he expressed fear and dismay that the revival of the Hebrew language might result in the spreading of a vogue that might lead to Christian love affairs with it; that Judaism itself might experience a revival together with its literature. And he cried out: "... a pestilence, which could not be considered more hostile and more dangerous for the teachings of Christ." [9] In the same breath he recommended to his friend to devote all of his time to the study of Greek rather than to "that Hebrew."

Wolgang Capito, the first reform preacher in Strassburg, did not mind being seen with Jews or meeting them socially for the purpose of study. One of his best friends was the famous Jew, Josel of Rosheim, whom Selma Stern called "The Leader of Jewry in the Holy Roman Empire of the German Nation." Capito and Josel came from Hagenau, the "City of Tolerance," where both men had spent their early youth. Anrich, in his *Strassburger Reformation*, characterized him as "mild, sincere, by nature leaning toward melancholy, in his more undogmatic manner the most generous of all German Reformers, a defender of the persecuted and suppressed. He remained true to the ideals of the first years of the Reformation, when everywhere else the confessional discord split the movement.... He was a friend of

Johann Reuchlin.

Erasmus and a mystic, siding closely with the Anabaptists and their millenarian hope of Christ's rule on Earth,"[10] a profound expert and lover of the Hebrew language, which he taught at the newly founded School of Sages in Strassburg, a busy collector of Hebrew books and manuscripts.[11]

Erasmus' anger climaxed with curses against the Jews, their Talmud and their Kabbala, forgetting that these two works were the educational sources of the Jewish people. Even the Church was reprimanded for paying too much attention to the Old Testament.[12]

B. B. Wolman, addressing himself to the type of tantrum such as Erasmus displayed again and again, has this to say: "Regression is at the core of every neurosis. An adult who reacts to frustration with a temper tantrum or helpless dispair reacts in a neurotic way."[13] Max Brod, while not a historian, had perhaps a keener psychological insight. He suspected that Erasmus' ambiguity about Hebrew favored scornful ignorance of that tongue *(ista lingua)* altogether. One gets the impression that he indeed prided himself to understand no more than just the rudiments. Charles Bené in his *Erasme et Saint Augustin* stated essentially the same view: "The reservations which Erasmus has about the study of Hebrew give evidence of similar scruples. He leaves this study to the Hebraists and the Jews. The reasons which he gives for this merit analysis: 'This language is not very widespread and, as it seems, is not sufficiently well-known among the Hebrews themselves; at the same time, I fear that a child, by studying this literature, may become impregnated with Judaism.' One knows that Erasmus had very early understood the usefulness of Hebrew. But, persuaded that one man cannot be proficient in everything, he abstained from it very quickly. Other reasons diverted him from it. Its usefulness seemed to him too limited. He did not esteem the usefulness of the Old Testament (as an instrument for a broad, public and Christian education) very highly. On the other hand, despite his friendship with Reuchlin, whose defender he also became, he remained rather indifferent toward certain hazardous assumptions of Hebrew philosophy, being himself reserved in the face of certain speculations. This distrust which existed already among the Church Fathers is found again in Vives *De Tradendis*

Disciplinis (Cologne, Gymn, 1136, p. 474), for instance, who suspected the Jews of having falsified the manuscripts, or simply of having neglected the tradition. Reasons of convenience, since he was in a hurry to proceed to essential matters and religious reasons, since he acts to protect himself from Judaism. Augustine experienced the same scruples."[14]

Erasmus indeed was alarmed by the thought that the propagation of Hebrew learning might seduce good Christians to become enamored with that alien Faith, might affect them like a bad virus and might even lure a few people away from the True Religion. Said he in a letter to Capito: "the restoration of Hebrew learning may give occasion to a revival of Judaism. This would be a plague as much to be opposed to the doctrine of Christ as anything that could happen."[15] What Erasmus was saying in the final analysis was this: Humanism is not for Jews. The ancient Greeks would have called his behavior "atae"—a foolish, god-implanted, unreasoning passion. We shall return to this issue again later on.

Other Humanists, fortunately for the development of interest in the Hebrew language, did not share Erasmus' studied ambiguity. "Ridiculing his intellectual dullness" (Beschraenktheit), as Otto Kluge called it,[16] they employed the services of Matthew Adrian (Matthaeus Adrianus), the wandering professor. His name became so famous that he taught Hebrew in Tuebingen, Heidelberg, Basel, Loewen, and Wittenberg. He was born of Jewish parents in Spain. In the aftermath of the expulsion of the Jews from Spain, he converted and after studies received a Doctor of Medicine degree. Like Joseph Hacohen, who did not convert, he moved about in Germany and Italy practicing medicine and earned money on the side by teaching Hebrew. We meet him again as a teacher of Pellican and his friend Reuchlin in Tuebingen in 1512. In a letter of introduction to Erasmus' publisher, Johannes Amerbach called him "the most profound and erudite of Hebraists in Germany."[17] Erasmus then wrote a note to Peter Gillis in October, 1517, in which he recommended Adrian for a position of Hebrew Professor at the University of Louvain. Showing his condescension in recommending a Jew, he called him "a Hebrew with an extraordinary knowledge of his proper tongue ... as if ebriety had not been common enough already, and Dorpius is leader of the Hebrew faction."[18] The editor F. M. Nichols comments: "... We should scarcely have expected to find Erasmus condescending to pun on the words 'ebrius' and 'Hebraeus'... But such was the Humanist mood: to show off Humanist sophistication at all cost, even if that pun hurt others." Perhaps we ought to translate *ebriety* as intoxication and not as drunkenness. Did Erasmus mean to equate Hebrews with a race of drunks, rather than a God-intoxicated People?

Adrian in his lectures stressed that Hebrew was the source of all languages and that all others derived from it—even Phoenician and Egyptian. This view was shared by the professors of Sturm who had a kind of puritanical aversion to the Greek fashion of the time. Once in the moderate intellectual climate of Louvain University, Adrian called the students of Hebrew "insane lovers of languages" (*insanos linquarum amatores*)![19] This seemingly implied that the tri-lingual humanist approach had caught on. After his stay in Wittenberg, where even Martin Luther fell under his spell for a fleeting moment, Adrian disappeared from the sight of historians.

It was Reuchlin, and to a degree Adrian, who can be called the true renewers of Hebrew studies, men who aspired to elevate Humanist linguistics from a vogue to a scientific program. From that time on Hebrew was studied not only in the synogogue and Jewish academies but also in colleges of western Europe. This is the man (*i.e.* Reuchlin) who wrote to his brother Dionysius: "I bequeath to you the fruit of my labors. I mourn the expulsion of the Jews from Spain, which could have had the total demise of the Hebrew language and Old Testament studies as a consequence. I beseech you and all young students not to allow yourselves to be troubled, but to search through the immeasurable abyss of this Science."[20] The true measure of Reuchlin's sincerity regarding Hebrew and Talmudic studies lies in the fact that both he and Melanchthon had issued one hundred copies of the Hebrew Bible and made them accessible to their students—in those days still quite a costly experiment. The universities in Tuebingen and in Wittenberg bore the costs. But other German universities were not as progressive. "The theologians of Cologne neither understood the Kabbala nor the Talmud. However, they were convinced that only Devil's works could hide behind them. They have to this day epigones, who have equally limited knowledge but greater power—means of persecution at their disposal."[21]

Renaissance Humanism was eclectic: Reuchlin's dependence on earlier Hebrew sources and scholars makes that clear. These men and their colleagues were fully conscious of their indebtedness to the Jewish past. But obviously, they all suffered from the medieval dilemma which psychologically accepted *and* rejected at one and the same time Jewish traditions and mores. It was this unrequited love affair which so many humanists were unable to resolve. From the historic vantage point we encounter these men in an area of exploration: the new printing press, the New World and new inventions, the search for a new identity—all of these provoked currents and crosscurrents, which were "aggravated" by the mere presence of the Jews,[22] including the intra-Christian ferment and the drifting toward the occult: Jewish Mysticism, The Kabbala. This drift was perhaps the most profound expression of Renaissance pessimism in which man saw the gulf between himself, God, and the World widen to almost "unredeemable" proportions.

In Judaism, Mysticism strives in general for a vital intensive contact with the Divinity, and this desire for an immediate awareness of, and communion with, God is basic. To the Kabbalist the Bible was full of miraculous stories, prophecies, and hidden words which almost defied the human mind. To them there was an air of mystery and secretive goings on that hovered between the holy pages of The Book of Books. Two main problems remained seemingly unanswered: Who is God, what is His essence?, and secondly: What is Creation? Ezechiel's visions and the Creation Story in the first chapters of Genesis thus became the focal point of Kabbalistic yearning for Truth and Understanding. Philo, the Alexandrian Jew, who had drunk from the cup of neo-Platonism, the Talmudists of Babylon and Palestine — all of them spoke of the Hidden Word of God in a pious whisper. It was not until the beginning of the fourteenth Century that Raymond Lullus (1232-1315) began to delve into the secret science of the Jews. Originally this rather eccentric man had undertaken to convert Moslems by making journeys to the Near East, and founding a

118   The Tragedy of Erasmus

college to teach missionaries the languages and literature of this area. He also wrote some three hundred esoteric works and only belatedly arrived at Jewish Kabbalism, obviously disappointed by the results of his mission to the Moslems. His was an exercise in Theosophy: he regarded the study of the Kabbala as a divine science and a veritable revelation of God to man. Lullus, the orthodox Christian, detected in the Jewish teachings the Trinitarian doctrine, the Coming of the Messiah, Original Sin, and others. He thus became the first great late Medieval synthesizer: the Kabbala confirmed the truth of Christianity. Conversely, synthesis offered him the means of attacking Judaism and a technique with which to persuade Jews to convert to the True Faith, Christianity. It does not surprise us to witness the persecution of Lullus by the orthodox establishment. However, the *Apology* in which he summarized his philosophy in forty-six sentences found favor in the eyes of Pope Alexander VI, and on June 18, 1493, Lullus was cleared of all charges of heresy. By indirection, of course, the study of the Kabbala and its disciples had also obtained clearance.[23] It was a triumph of Faith and Reason over Catholic superstition and intransigence toward Judaic studies in the New Age. Thus Johannes Reuchlin has a precursor who, as he thought, had paved the way for him and his study of the Kabbala.

Pico della Mirandola, the Italian Kabbalist, was another precursor. If moderns were to type Pico della Mirandola, they might call him a religious enthusiast. His Hebrew library numbered more than one hundred manuscripts, which was considerable if one recalls that Pope Urban V at Avignon owned just about as many as this overpowering, brilliant, and mysterious figure.[24]
Born into the aristocracy, he was related to the most important princely families of Italy. Padua, Bologna, and Paris, the capital of the scholastic world, were his main stops on the road to a humanist education. Typical of his time, his intellectual hunger was voracious. He even made an attempt to summarize all of mankind's heretofore achieved knowledge in a new *Summa* that was to advance Humanist culture throughout Europe. Pope Innocent VIII thought him presumptuous and tried to impound him and his work, and Pico fled to France where he was

incarcerated outside Paris (Vincennes). He later managed to flee with the help of his friends, finding a place of refuge at the Florentine Academy that was sponsored by the Medici. There he came under the influence of the hothead Savonarola and began to live the life of a devout Christian. When Charles VIII, the French expansionist King, entered Florence, it spelled the end of Pico's career.

It is remarkable that Pico studied Hebrew in the open and without any pretenses. His teachers were two Levantine Jewish scholars: Johann Alemanno from Constantinople and Del Medigo from Crete. It was from these two men that Reuchlin became also a devotee of the Kabbala, the great book of Mysticism. They believed that behind all religious and philosophical experiences and speculation lay unity as expressed in Christianity. Thus, the assimilation of "Greek and Hebrew learning could in the long run only redound to the purification of Christianity."[25] We see how humanist scholarship was put into the service of the Catholic Church, which did not appreciate these efforts, and at the same time served as an inspiration to other Christian Humanists. To this day, Pico's treatises, such as his *Apology*, the *Heptaplus*, and some of his other metaphysical writings give testimony to a genuinely open mind which always, as in the title of his book, proclaimed *The Dignity of Man*. Erasmus had no sense of history. He was hindered by his medieval heritage. His Humanism, which was Christian first and foremost, was faithbound and at best strove to accommodate classical ideals with those of the New Testament. His type of religious amalgam was hemmed in on both sides by piety and faith. And this tragic stance put Erasmus outside historical consciousness and stationed him where Martin Luther stood all his life. Even the dry Englishman, John Colet, had fallen under Pico's spell, and by 1517 Colet admitted that he too had fallen victim to Kabbalism. In a letter to Erasmus he revealed that he had read Reuchlin's *De Arte Cabalistica*.

Adaptation is the key work to understand what the Christian Kabbalist tried to achieve: he substituted the Christ-had-come-theory (Messiah) for the vagueness of the Jewish Mashiakh of the future. And he adapted the literal interpretation of the Holy Scriptures to the speculative techniques of the Kabbala for the discovery of Christian implications and verities. The three highest heavenly spheres (*sefiroth*): crown, wisdom, and understanding (keter, khokhmah, and binah) became a New Trinity: keter was equated with The Father, khokhmah with The Logos, and binah with Divine Grace, and Tifereth (glory), the sixth of the Sefiroth, became the Jesus Incarnate.

Thus to Reuchlin, the Kabbala had become a new way of life. Each word had meaning. It was, in Martin Buber's terminology, holy (a sacrament). Beyond that, each comma and dot had a hidden, inner meaning, as both Jews and Christians agreed. Believing further that each consonant of the Hebrew alphabet had a higher numerical connotation, the Kabbalist—of whatever faith—could open with these keys the gates of knowledge, the kingdom of Heaven. Thus, the entire Hebrew language, its vowels, consonants and dots, its words and numbers were the true Representatives of the Holy One himself. He revealed himself through them and laid open to man His plan of salvation, which remained hidden to those who do not know, and hence cannot grasp God's design. Therefore, it was the pious, and he alone, who could partake of God's secrets and be enabled to persevere. It was this inner understanding of the Talmud and the Kabbala that Reuchlin, who became involved in this controversy with Erasmus and the Inquisitors, would not surrender at any price. It is here that Reuchlin agreed with the Jews who postulated: "We Jews are not accustomed to use language with frills. For we have learned under the blows of the whips to talk simply—without frills. We seek the truth of a problem more than the ornamentation of language."[26] As much as Reuchlin and others, who were the erstwhile enemies of the Jews, came to display a deep and genuine affection for their culture, they came away from them in the knowledge that the Jews were "the well of all wisdom, and taskmaster of all the nations."

As we have seen, Erasmus had very little respect for these Jewish speculations. Underhandedly, he sent Reuchlin's copy of his *On the Kabbalistic Art* to John Fisher, Bishop of Rochester, possibly for further comment or to discredit his great rival. At any rate, Colet found this out and wrote Erasmus a sharp note: "I am somewhat angry with you for another reason, too; you sent

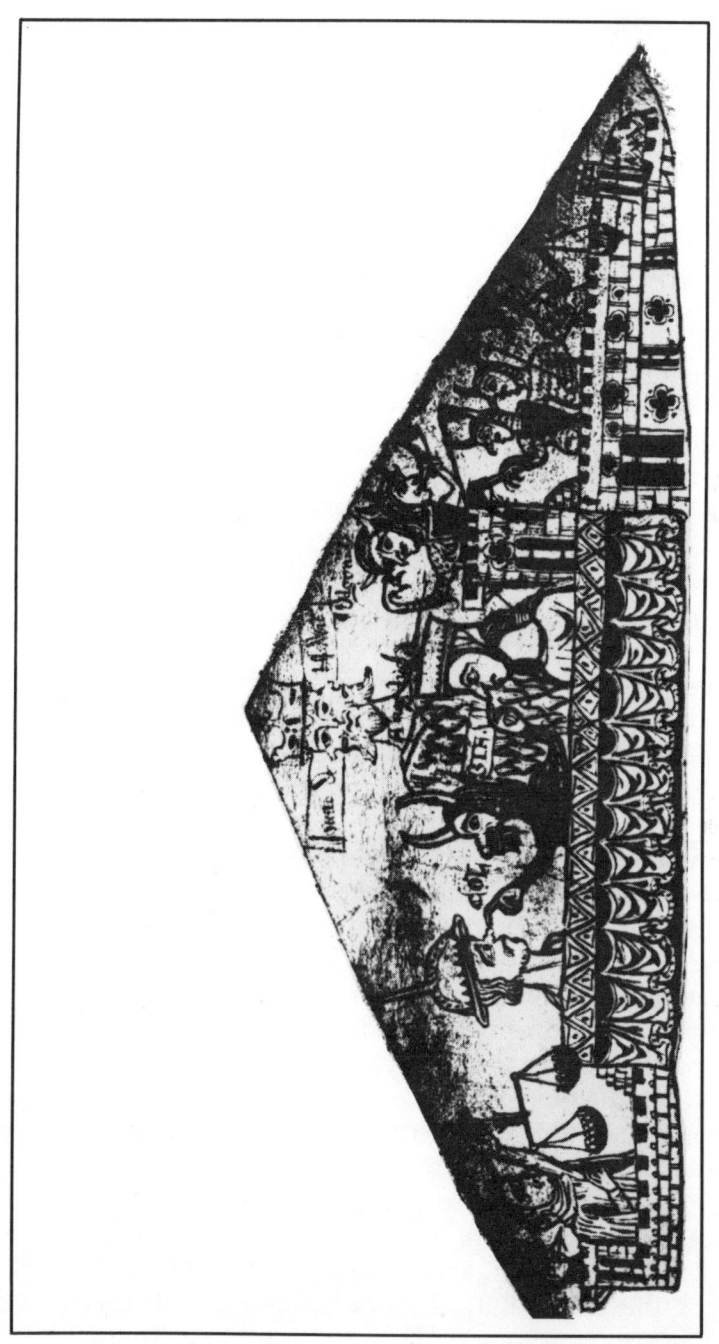

The Forces of Hell Tormenting a Jew.

Reuchlin's book on Kabbala to Rochester, and not to me. Not that I would not want it sent to him; but I wish you had sent one copy to me at the same time. For I take such pleasures in your love that I suffer when I see you less mindful of me than of others. That book came into my hands first, and it was read by me before it was given to Rochester. I dare not evaluate the book. I know my own ignorance and how blind I am about matters so remote and the works of such a man. As I read, however, much of it seemed to me to be greater miracles of words than of deeds; for (as it shows) I know not what mysteries Hebrew words have in their characters and combinations. Erasmus, my friend, of such books and of knowledge there is no end."[27] So we see that Colet did not regret to have been introduced to the world of the Kabbala. And as for Fisher, he too got a smattering of this wholly new field and at least got a faint idea that this oral tradition was as important to the Jews as their revealed Scriptures.

Thus, the Kabbala, the esoteric school of Jewish religious thought, dating back to Moses of Leon, the thirteenth Century Castilian Jew who wrote the *Zohar* (Splendor), became part of the sixteenth century Humanist's inventory and repertoire. However, when the Humanists tried their hand in missionizing Jews they had little success. Guilliaum Postell would be another case in point where a Christian Kabbalist became deeply concerned with the identity-crisis of Christianity. Like Erasmus he was deeply concerned with the spectre of Christian disunity which he saw as a world-wide theological conflict. After all, two or more new churches had broken away from the old; meanwhile, Islam was making great inroads into Central and Southern Europe. To top it all, alien cultures, including Judaism, began to divert attention from Christian traditions and beliefs. And, the whole non-Christian world was watching the inner convulsion of western Christendom. Already in the Central Middle Ages, Pope Gregory VII in one of his letters, made this poignant observation: "I declare to you that the true Christian faith as taught to us by our fathers through the son of God descending from Heaven, is turned over to the evil fashions of this world and is alas...almost annihilated. Its ancient colors are changed, and it has become the laughingstock, not only of the Devil, but of Jews, Saracens, and pagans."[28]

Almost in desperation did Postell and other Christian mystics begin to believe that a Kabbalistic approach might offer a solution out of the Christian dilemma. Perhaps as a new type of all-embracing remedy, that could bring into harmony Greek and Jewish thoughts "reason and authority, nature and grace. . . . By making truth communicable, Kabbala made it applicable to the solution of human problems." [29]

We must assume that during Erasmus' lifetime some people close to him recognized his duplicity—what some writers called The Enigma of Erasmus. In a private conversation between Luther and Frederick the Wise, his protector and friendly jailer in October, 1520, Frederick asked the Reformer's opinion of Erasmus. Luther's epigrammatic reply was: "What a wonderful little man that is. . . ." Then there was a pause. And he continued: "Erasmus is an eel. Only Satan can grab him!" [30] There is a tragic note in this comment, coming from a great man who failed to make friends with one of the brightest minds of his time.

NOTES

[1] R. Agricola, *Nonnulla Opuscula* (Basel, 1518), p. 63.
[2] Quoted by L. Geiger in *Renaissance and Humanism in Italy and Germany* (Berlin, 1882), p. 507.
[3] J. Reuchlin, *Rudimenta Hebraica* (Pforzheim, 1506).
[4] Welzig, *Erasmus' Letters*, Vol. I, 405, pp. 35-37.
[5] Welzig, Vol. II, 50 ff. Here are some samples: In the *On Mending the Peace of the Church* he translated the Hebrew term Judah with "confess" (p. 363); the word Cedar (eres) with "darkness" (p. 353) and Sebaoth (Ts'vaot) with "power" (p. 346).
[6] J. A. Faulkner: *Erasmus The Scholar* (Eaton, 1907), p. 188.
[7] Jerome Busleiden, brother of a former archbishop of Besancon, and himself a councillor of the King of Spain.
[8] W. Welzig, *Erasmus of Rotterdam, Selected Writings*, Vol. III (Darmstadt, 1967), p. 140 ff.
[9] Welzig, *Letters*, Vol. II, 491, pp. 137-39.
[10] Chiliastic = millenarian, *i.e.*, a span of one thousand years of holiness during which Christ is to rule on Earth (Revelations 20:1-5).
[11] Selma Stern, *Josel of Rosheim* (Stuttgart, 1959), p. 126.
[12] Welzig, *Letters*, Vol. III, p. 253.
[13] Benjamin B. Wolman, "Sense and Nonsense in History," *The Psychoanalytic Interpretation of History* (New York, 1971), p. 108.
[14] Charles Bené, *Erasme et Saint Augustin* (Geneva, 1969), p. 367.
[15] Erasmus to Capito in a letter dated: Antwerp, 2/26/1516.
[16] *Die Hebraische Sprachwissenschaft in Deutschland im Zeitalter des Humanismus*, Zeitschrift des Jüdischen Denkens, Vol. III (Berlin, 1931), p. 91.
[17] Quoted by L. Geiger, p. 151, in *Briefweschel* (Berlin, 1882), p. 151.
[18] See Erasmus letters: 656, 658, 660, 661-63.
[19] Letter dedicated to Spalatin, p. 1 b and Kluge, *Humanismus*, p. 24.
[20] O. Kluge, p. 94, re: March 7, 1506.
[21] Richard Friendental, p. 137.
[22] Joseph Leon Blau, *The Christian Interpretation of the Kabbala in the Renaissance* (Columbia, 1944), p. 14 ff.
[23] Geiger, Ludwig: *J. Reuchlin, Sein Leben und Seine Werke* (Leipzig, 1871).
[24] M. P. Gilmore in his *The World of Humanism* (Harvard, 1963), p. 195.
[25] *Ibid.*, p. 197.
[26] As quoted by Wilhelm Maurer in the *Theologisch Literarische Zeitung* (1952) #9, pp. 538-540.
[27] Allen, *Erasmus Letters*, Vol. II, #599.
[28] Marshall W. Baldwin, *Christianity Through the 13th Century* (New York), p. 186.
[29] W. J. Bouwsma, *Postel and the Significance of Renaissance Cabalism* (Washington, 1959), p. 263.
[30] Robert H. Murray, *Luther and Erasmus* (London, 1920).

8
The Probe

The Physical Profile

Erasmus was in poor health most of his life. As a young boy in Holland he had recurring attacks of quartan malaria,[1] and in later years was plagued by kidney and bladder stones (renal and visical calculi), stomach troubles, dysentery, and many bouts with infectious, painful inflammation of the genitals (lymphogranuloma). Professor A. Werthemann, pathologist of the University of Basel, who examined his exhumed body in June, 1928, came to the conclusion that Erasmus was also suffering from syphilis, possibly contracted when on his journey to Louvain. This type of pandemic syphilis was quite common in the later part of the Fifteenth and all through the Sixteenth Centuries.[2] Arthritis seemed to have also handicapped him, and in August, 1514, he had attacks of blood spitting.

Emotionally as well as physically, Erasmus was unwell. Dr. V. W. D. Schenk, a Dutch psychiatric authority, examined his letters and concluded that Erasmus was a hypochondriac and a neurotic and that he had an emotional, volatile nature and that he was psychasthenic.[3] "The latter is a neurotic condition which is marked by a sense of inadequacy, unreality, anxiety, and doubt, and also a neurosis characterized by obsessions, phobias, tics, and compulsions.... There may also be associated restlessness, palpitation, fatigue, or irritability; and a definite sense of dread or fear.... The anxiety is rationalized, as a fear of syphilis, cancer, insanity, or contamination, among many others. Obsessions and phobias may occur at the onset or during the course of other diseases, notably schizophrenia. Frequently, obsessive impulses dominate behavior. These may be peculiar (touching lampposts, avoiding lines on sidewalk), or distinctly antisocial. In the latter event, it is indicative of a condition more serious than a neurosis."

Dr. Schenk's findings speak for themselves and support our thesis: Erasmus was a sick man. And, burdened with illegitimacy, which he never overcame, his mind became warped, insecure and full of built-in contradictions. Schenk's definition of psychasthenia thus underscores the theologian Rupp's evaluation of Erasmus which concluded that "he was always moved by intellectual appetites and dislikes, and we may suppose he made little effort to understand [himself]."[4] Our medical definition appears as if it had been written with an eye on Erasmus.

Inadequacy was a prominent feature of Erasmus' neuroticism. Living with his illegitimacy was uncomfortable and it even prompted him at one time to solicit the aid of the Pope himself. In response Pope Leo X wrote to his Collector and notary, Andreas Ammonius: "[Erasmus] labors under a defect of birth, having been begotten of an illicit and, as he fears, incestuous and forbidden intercourse."[5]

Erasmus' compulsive letter writing to all sorts of people may have been a cover-up to chase away the fears and doubts about his "friends." To lose them caused anxiety as well as ambiguity. Hence, his vacillating performances, his ups and downs, trying to hold on to them or to betray them. He was never sure of himself. This may be one reason why he travelled from one place to the other, never trying to root himself, let alone commit himself. He was the most restless of Humanists, driven as it were, by his own admission, by the Devil or by his bad conscience. His irritability comes clearly to the fore as one studies his correspondence. The exchange of letters with James Battus is a good example: he is trying to use his so-called friend to woo the Marchioness Anna of Veere and to elicit a generous patronage from her. Besides the typical sycophantic aspect of the affair, it clearly reveals Erasmus' impatient irritability when Battus seemingly cannot perform.

Sir Thomas More. From a painting by Holbein, the Younger.

Before the mental eye the figure of the dying knight Ulrich Hutten appears again, the man who was unclean and syphylitic. Erasmus ejected him when he knocked at his door just months before his death: he feared contagion, just as he feared cholera and smallpox, a virus, or unclean linen in a hostelry. It is the response of a hypochondriac, although rationalized as in the case of his many trips to England. He was driven there by his empty purse, trying to capitalize on his famous name, to meet his soul-brothers: More, Colet, Fisher, and company. Yet, once he had filled out his sides again, he took off, blaming it on the bad weather or poor beer. Some may also regard his religious attitudes as obsessive. One gets the feeling that he somehow scrambled all over the theological map, seeking for a religious answer to satisfy not only the needs of the time in which he lived, but also his own. He vacillated between orthodoxy and reform, conformity and humanism. This is why historians have difficulty in placing him: some see him as a devout Catholic, others as an agnostic, á la Voltaire. Some regard him as cleverly impious, while some call him the Great Synthesizer. We know that Erasmus was mentally ill: hovering between friendships and betrayal of friends. Antisocial at times, at others he would be charming and endearing. Fearful of commitment and unsure of himself, he could be both persuasive and elusive, generous, and miserly, "a great master of compromise and mildness . . . who was often plagued by a morbid persecution-fear."[6] He was also a beggar and a snob, a Christian and a pagan, Catholic and Protestant, all rolled into one. He could be loving and full of hate, an intolerant zealot and an angelic man of compassion, screaming against Jews and yet pleading for the establishment of a Chair of Hebrew studies. A man for all seasons, a weathervane for all climes. As early as 1899, Harvard Professor Ephraim Emerton arrived at this most interesting observation: "He was already showing that joy in the idea of being persecuted which later seems to have reacted on his memory of his earliest years. It flattered his vanity to think that men cared enough about him to abuse him, and such abuse gave him an added claim upon the devotion of his friends. His nature demanded affection and admiration, and he was ready to repay them in kind, so long as he thereby incurred no lasting or burdensome obligation."[7] Or did he have a sense of self-destructiveness, let us say like Socrates or his real idol, Jesus? Was an ultimate martyrdom really one way of achieving genuine identity and recognition? This writer is not impressed with Erasmus' "sacrifices." History is full of personalities who were willing to give their lives for an idea. As B. B. Wolman observed: "The idea of self-sacrifice and service for others is rooted in parenthood, but it may transcend it and encompass entire mankind." He then cites examples, such as Christ, Giordano Bruno, and others who preferred death to life. Into this category also belonged Rabbi Akiba who accepted suffering for the Kiddush Hashem, the santification of His name. With Erasmus it was different: he may have "toyed" with the idea of self-sacrifice or supreme suffering—but he was too cowardly to accept this as a solution to as to what he conceived his role to be, namely the recognized spokesman for a revived Christianity, harking back to the ancient days of almost immaculate design.[8]

W. T. H. Jackson was most perceptive when he observed: "Like most humanists, Erasmus loved attacking the more obvious social weaknesses—flattery, chicanery, office-seeking, untruthfulness, false pride—but there is evidence in his letters that he was guilty of them all. Even if we make allowance for the different standards of the sixteenth century in these matters, we cannot entirely exculpate him. For many of these weaknesses his upbringing was to blame. It should not be forgotten that he had no family life. He felt the ignominy of his birth deeply and made desperate shifts to justify it. It would not be an exaggeration to say that he took refuge in letters. Throughout his life he had an almost desperate need for friendship which he took pains to conceal under an ironical attitude. Yet at the same time the circumstances of his youth left him with many of the characteristics of a recluse. So far as can be judged, few people ever secured a real hold on his affections."[9] Like his contemporary, Luther, he made untold friends throughout his long life but in the end he had alienated if not betrayed them all.

J. J. Mangan commends Erasmus to our pity and sympathy. In his book he analyzed his character from the point of view of a twentieth-century Humanist. He described him not as one in the fullness of his health "but as sensitive as a neurasthenic." Sigmund

Freud defined neurasthenia as "probably an expression of sexual frustration, which probably complicates the symptoms by an element of renunciation as well." One notices that Freud uses the term *probably* twice. Mangan rather concisely gives a picture of the Humanist, quoted here in excerpts: "He was sickly, often a thwarted genius, and that he was for the greater part self-taught. One can easily predict that he would bear most forms of mental stress, but poorly. His egoism . . . . brought upon him tribulations which he bore with frequent loss of dignity. . . . He could never learn the art of being eloquently silent."[11] "He had no tenderness of conscience, nor was he of a generous disposition. . . ." To an enemy who was without protection, like the Jews, Erasmus was merciless, while no one could surpass him in kindness and forbearance when the enemy was backed by influential and powerful friends, "then Erasmus must have been secretive, reserved, irritable, quick to resent imaginary or real slights, suspicious, hungering for sympathy and friendship but too proud to make the first advances, internally burning with envy of his more fortunate companions, and externally haughty with pride in his superior mental ability. . . . [In] his loneliness and desolation, in pure bitterness of spirit he resolved to excel not only them but the whole world, and to make a name for himself which the world would be compelled at least to honor and respect. . . . it is not surprising if the more generous impulses of his soul were in the course of time atrophied. . . . So we have a mind filled with resentment and envy, helpless to protect himself from insult, and envious of all who were more happily placed then he." And this included his former confreres. He sputters in his *Praise of Folly*,[12]

Coming nearest to these in felicity are the men who generally call themselves "the religious" and "monks"—utterly false names both, since most of them keep as far away as they can from religion and no people are more in evidence in every sort of place. But I do not see how anything could be more dismal than these monks if I did not succor them in many ways. For though people as a whole so detest this race of men that meeting one by accident is supposed to be bad luck, yet they flatter themselves to the queen's taste. For one thing, they reckon it the highest degree of piety to have no contact with literature, and hence they see to it that they do not know how to read. For another, when with asinine voices they bray out in church those psalms they have learned, by rote rather than by heart, they are convinced that they are annointing God's ears with the blandest of oil. Some of them make a good profit from their dirtiness.

Erasmian Hang-Ups

Throughout his literary career Erasmus showed a distinct dislike of Jews; he refused to mingle with them, let alone take Hebrew instruction from a qualified Jewish scholar. He distrusted them in fear that they might hurt the Church through insidious pacts with opponents of the Church. And he abhorred the thought that some Christian might fall victim to Jewish propaganda and convert to its superstition. Some psychologists will characterize this type of behavior, if fostered over the years and crystallized, as an overt and obsessive dislike. Our Humanist developed under the educational guidance of The Brethren of the Common Life, what can be termed Judeophobia—a combination of fear, hatred and contempt for Jews—and all this despite the fact that he did not know a Jew in all of his life, with the exception of the converted Pfefferkorn, whom he never encountered in person. The fear for the culture of his Church which he believed was threatened by the Jews, who allegedly gave the Reformation a forward push, and his religious contempt for those ritual-performing Jews gave him the kind of dormant contempt upon which he later elaborated and talked himself into a more violent form of antisemitism ("Europe has to become Judenrein"). Lastly, Erasmus was convinced that that International Jewry was plotting to destroy his Church. We may call this imaginary behavior paranoid or delusional.

Most modern historians agree that Erasmus showed this ambivalence throughout his life. His was the classical posture of a fence-sitter, who was inconsistent with his expressed views (on the Reformation, for instance) and who showed ambiguity toward his erstwhile friends, such as Reuchlin or Luther.[13] Love and hate were constantly interchanged by him as if they were complementary or necessary to each other. In Erasmus' view, the Jews had killed Jesus. For this they were the object of hate, although he was fully aware of the fact that Jesus did have an intimate relationship with them: He was a Jew from the day he was born until His death. "Lama asavtani," He is believed to have said on the cross:

"Why hast Thou forsaken me?" Erasmus' hate of the Jews turned into the love of Christ. If one adds to this that Erasmus needed a father desperately because he himself had no father-identity because of his illegitimate background, then we can appreciate his equally frantic effort to elevate Jesus to the New Father image. As long as he lived no harm was to come on the head of his newly won God-head, the Christ.

Whether Erasmus "repressed" his inner feelings about his savior, we do not know, although it is unlikely, for he grew up fast. But one thing we do know and that is that young children fear, love, and hate their fathers. And since the Jews were held responsible for the death of his adopted Father, he would "reap moral and psychological benefit in redemption from sin."[14] Thus the Jew became to the life of Erasmus essential not only for his individual type of Christianity but also as a scapegoat for his own personal sins. The Freudian psychologist would add at this point that on the unconscious level the crucified Jesus (Father) represented to him the culmination of the unconscious death wishes of his oedipal period.

There were also other bases for Erasmus' antisemitism: as he grew older he experienced a sense of deep inner embarrassment, unconscious and non-verbalized; and this he had in common with all Jew baiters in history: Christianity was a direct offshoot and close relative of Judaism. The Christ he worshipped was also a Jew. Should he hate or love, love or hate? So, here we are stopped again by Erasmus' ambiguity: he did have an attachment, however flimsy and vicarious, to the Old Testament and its people, though he made a studied effort not to understand them (as a child misunderstands a father when the child is in the wrong). It was his subconscious in which he expressed his feelings in a bitter mixture of admiration of hate and love, in an unbridgeable paranoia that haunted him all his life. His shifting attitude toward Hebraic studies at Louvain also showed both the attachment and obligation he felt toward this cursed race and his resentment of those Jew-Professors who were certainly worth a salary of seventy-five Ducats per year.

This behavior is common and normal. As for Erasmus he had studied Chrysostomos, who wrote that the Jews were traitors to

God and hence to be castigated, repudiated, and condemned—but not fully. The motive for a grudging love, or tolerant hatred, did not matter. It was the "Witness Theory," that believed in keeping the Jew alive to be the Christians' daily reminder of Jewish infamy, and it was Paul's saying that Christianity was a branch that had sprung from the tree of Judah. Erasmus and the Church, violent in their anti-Jewish behavior, also showed moments of reluctant tolerance.

There was one point, however, on which Erasmus did not compromise: just as he loved in an almost childlike way his adopted Father, and believed in Him, so would he cast his hatred upon anyone who denied or disbelieved Him. In this respect, Erasmus remained the obedient son of his Mother-Church, which demanded total submission to her will, and submission by extension to His (Jesus') will. Mother and Father were reunited! He would not and could not leave them. This obviates all efforts to tie him to the Reformation and it almost negates his Humanist posture: Christ had become a "projection into the Universe of the father-figure, of the father-son relationship and the super-ego—the heir to the Oedipus complex."[15]

Another question, of course, is this: did the ambivalency of Erasmus toward the Jews lead him also to an ambivalence toward God—now that he found his real Father? This writer leaves an answer to the Christian Theologians. After all: how can a Jew visiting a Church today distinguish between the imploratory "Oh God" and "Oh Lord"?—Who has priority: God or Christ? Or is God really dead in the Christian Churches? What is meant by this theological ambivalence? In the case of Erasmus we get a different impression: since his theology is Christ-centered, God the Father takes the low-road. As a matter of fact, the researcher will have no difficulty in detecting the almost studied underemphasis or neglect of God in Erasmus' religious tracts and literary discourses. Christ had replaced God in Erasmus' thinking. Without Him, He could not be. Erasmus was, of course, unaware of these difficulties in his time.[16]

The Jewish Ghost

One of the amazing phenomena that comes to us from the end

of the fourteenth century is that Jews were killed first and hated afterwards. The Jew was hated even when he was no longer seen, when he had been thrown out of several of the Western European countries.[17] Thus there were two Jews—psychologically speaking—that upset men like Erasmus: the mythical Jew and the contemporary Jew. Both were needed by an insecure and missionary Church who fitted them into her theological scenario. Unfortunately for the Jews at the time of German Humanism, this type of Judeophobia seemed to depend for nourishment more "on the substratum on which the national culture rested." The Jew became the Church's object of cheap propaganda, a carricature, a Christ-devouring, almost apocalyptic male-animal that corralled the lowly and superstitious Christians back into the dark halls of the Cathedrals. The mystique of the Jew became the fetter of the frightened and submissive, protected by the mighty arms of the Mother Church. Thus, Germany became eminently qualified for Jew-hatred, as it was culturally more primitive than England, Spain, or the Netherlands. We direct the reader's attention to the many obscene plays, satires or Church-dramas—such as Chaucer's *Prioress' Tale*, Sebastian Brant's *Ship of Fools*, and Erasmus' *Julius Exclusus*, the anti-Jewish classics, and the Oberammergauer Passion plays, including Erasmus' own sarcastic references to the Jews, which delighted the German masses and their indwelling barbaric ethnic streak. This is the reason why we have called German Humanism the Teutonic version of its Italian counterpart. If one adds to this the development of trade which now became worldwide due to overseas discoveries, the Jew became increasingly "international." He was disliked by the have-nots, the poor, plague-ridden masses, who needed the "usurer-Jew" as an emotional outlet for their own plight. In the writings of Erasmus, all of these motives—economic, religious, political, or national—melt into one. Perhaps this explains why men such as he and Luther were "anti-capitalistic," that in their view money indeed was the root of all evil. It distracted the Christian from being a Christian. Or was it, as far fetched as it may seem, because their savior was betrayed by a handful of silver-pieces? One wonders. However, we may have here an amalgamation of feelings that created an ever intensified hatred. Now the reader understands what Erasmus meant when he cried out in his letters repeatedly: "If it is Christian to hate Jews, we are all Christians in full measure!"

After this anguished outburst, we can hardly be surprised when Ulrich Hutten joined him with equal vigor and sick Germanic lustiness. Self-righteously he moaned, "Germany could not have produced such a monster [as Pfefferkorn]. His parents are Jews, and he remains such, even if he has plunged his unworthy body into the baptism of Christ."[18] "As for the venerable Erasmus," said the French writer Leon Poliakov, "he was scarcely less 'racist', to use our current terminology...."[19]

If this constant intellectual agitation by Church and literati in general became the vogue of the day, is it wonder that Jews were disliked? Brainwashing, as it were, has became again a modern tool to incite the masses and to keep them in line, as Hitler and Stalin proved so disastrously. State censorship of books unfriendly to a regime, or the Index of the Church, are separated by only a few hundred years. And the book burning is another variant. The added dimension was this: by burning books, the Jew was also destroyed in effigy.

In spite of the cynicism in our time, we humans have come a long way since Erasmus' tragic encounter with the Jews. To the humanist today the words of Jacques Maritain sound like an affirmation of Faith for all mankind in which the Jew plays perhaps a God-ordained role. In his superb prose he wrote: "We see in Israel's suprahuman relation to the world ... a kind of reversed analogy to the Church. Israel, we believe, is assigned, in the order of temporal history and its own finalities, a work of terrestrial activation of the world's body ... it does not leave the world in repose; it keeps it from sleeping; it teaches the world to be discontent and uneasy so long as it does not have God; it stimulates the movement of history."[20]

Emotional and Sexual Disorders

What Eric Erikson calls *The* Event (in a person's psychological development) was in Erasmus' life his illegitimacy or even his awareness of being perhaps of incestual background. It was a deeply formative experience that molded his character, his attitude toward people, and it came to haunt him like a bad dream. It affected his health and mental and sexual stability. Thus, his psychological make-up had to evolve from his early youth "fantasy-relationship-systems" that produced an intensity of feeling in the inner self.[21] Inner pressures and the actualization of those pressures were the result. One of them was his constant anxiety. Its chief characteristic was that it was normally unorganized, diffuse and all pervasive. In Erasmus it combined a conscious dread and fear, manifesting itself in various forms of discomfort and admitted disability. Wherever he went, he felt uncomfortable, fearful of disease and perceiving all sorts of immediate dangers, such as contagion and the plague. It was this shadow of the unknown which was Erasmus' constant travelling companion.

Another factor within his fantasy-relationship system was his inability to come to grips with what we call authority. The Church would be one, the teachings of the Church Fathers another. The Pope or the Christ, the Old or the New Testament were yet other authorities. If we add to this Erasmus' fears that people imposed on him professionally or otherwise, his imaginary feeling of getting hurt physically, these factors may have even produced an idea-fixation of becoming impotent. Erasmus displayed these characteristics to a full measure. We could call it an exaggerated sense of vulnerability.

In our evaluation of Erasmus, he appears beset both by all sorts of fears which he cannot overcome by himself (in the absence of friends or a "psychiatrist") and by the self-realization of his total impotence in the intellectual as well as his physical worlds. Neither as a Humanist nor a man was he capable of performing (and reacting) normally and convincingly—not even amongst his contemporaries. A similar analysis of another antisemite was expressed by Psychologist Walter C. Langer, in a book on Hitler. Uncannily, much of Hitler's trouble we can redetect in Erasmus, the antisemite of four hundred years ago. In Hitler's case, "the Jew had become for him the symbol of sex, disease and his [own] perversion, and the masochist he really was, he derived a vicarious pleasure from the suffering of others in whom he could see himself."

This historian is tempted to compare these two personalities, Hitler and Erasmus: Hitler was a neurotic psychopath "probably bordering on schizophrenia." Fear dominated all his life, fears of all kinds, from sickness to death itself. He was an Erasmus without learning but with enormous power. But then Langer goes on to tell us that Hitler suspected that his real grandfather was Jewish. Could it possibly be that Erasmus too had such fears and apprehensions? After all, he bemoaned again and again his illegitimacy, he wept especially over the fate of Spanish Christendom that had been polluted by Jewish blood (marranos). Could it be that he harbored subconsciously those fears too? Was he, too, of Jewish descent or fearful that members of his immediate family could possibly be, or become embarrassed by, an admixture of Jewish blood? These are some of the questions we must ask, although we must be equally honest in admitting that it is almost impossible, in retrospect, to come up with certainties. To Erasmus the world assumed proportions of great evil, if not hostility. It was the danger of the Unknown that he feared. The Jew qualified eminently as a sinister Unknown and became the dark and uncanny enemy. And Erasmus clung to him tenaciously and irrationally as the root of all his own evil. It is the pattern common to all antisemitism. The Jew was Erasmus' enemy within and without. It was what behavior psychologists have named the Psychodynamics of Jew-hatred. We call Erasmus' attitude (or Hitler's disposition) compensatory and pathological. Religiously, Erasmus was convinced of the superiority of all that was Christian and the inferiority of all that was subhuman, *i.e.* Jewish. In Hitler it took on the form of Aryan superiority. But what was he (Erasmus or Hitler) to do about his suspicion of being of possibly Jewish origin? In both men, the quest for a non-Jewish antecedents could not be satisfied. It compelled each one to prove that he (Erasmus or Hitler) was racially pure by persecuting Jews to the ultimate limit. This is the reason why Erasmus never talked about his family—but neither did Hitler. By the same token, Erasmus had to prove to himself that he did not fear his real or imaginary enemies.

Another problem Erasmus faced was that of coming to grips with his Self. It confused him no end. He is at once ostentatiously superior with his humanist rivals such as Reuchlin, Stunica, or Pico, and then—although not openly admitted—inferior. To cite one example: Erasmus was always in need of money and this time he had chosen the Marchioness Anna Borsselen as an object of his sycophantism. He wrote to his friend Battus "I am not a little in dread of a Court, but I am very conscious of my unlucky star." And then he went on to tell him how to get from her money, horses, precious diamonds, and even a position, while he stood fearfully aside, letting his friend do the bidding. Unsuccessful, lacking even a semblance of modesty or humility he wrote again: "Then persuade her (Anna) to look out for some Church living for me, so that when I come back, I may have a quiet place to devote myself to my books;" and "every man of genius found his Maecenas."[22] Ackerman and Jahoda, the psychologists, express this Erasmian "technique" the following way: "These feelings of inner doubt and ambivalence toward one's own self are frequently too painful to be accepted without compensatory efforts. Inferiority, weakness, dependency, a tendency toward compulsive submissiveness and basic passivity, are often concealed from the world and even from one's own consciousness. The apparent substitute for such awareness is a tendency toward compensatory self-aggrandizement."[23]

One of the striking manifestations of a confusing self-image is the tendency toward homosexuality. Erasmus, the ex-priest, had two papal dispensations, from Julius II and from Leo X, allowing him to doff his monastic garb and to feel no longer bound by priestly restrictions. He indeed showed inclinations toward homosexuality, or at least fear of this type of sexual behavior. It may have goaded him to fight against the authority of his superiors. Psychoanalysts have observed "that antisemitism and homosexuality are related only to the extent that they are expressions of the same basic conflict: the confusion of one's own identity and struggle with one's own passivity." Both of these types are confused about their identity.

Erasmus wrote many endearing letters to his male friends. And it is astonishing to find the total absence of an intimate correspondence with women, even with his own mother. And we do not know of any love affairs that could have enlivened Erasmus' lonely life. He also never referred to the medieval Marian Cult.[24] Yet, when he wrote about women his otherwise flawless expressions became almost clumsy, as if he were made uncomfortable even to mention women. The letter to his friend James Battus is a case in point. "I count her, the Marchioness Anna Borsselen," he said, "not among common women, but among those of *manly* qualities." Then Erasmus gets to the point "If I were not so *awfully fond of* you, Battus, my dear fellow, so that to *live with you* would repay me for any inconvenience, these things might turn me from my plans." This remark of Erasmus hastened the author, Ephraim Emerton, to observe: "This letter is one of the most important revelations of Erasmus' methods of providing for himself .... Erasmus speaks especially of a settled life of study, with *Battus as the chief attraction....* It is not a guileless youth ... but a man of the world conscious of himself to the point of morbidity, and yet willing to go pretty far along the road of sycophancy to the great."[25] In a follow-up letter, Erasmus waxed indignant, showing his low opinion of "that Lady" and Battus himself: "And finally you lament the hard fortune of your mistress. You seem to me to be ailing with *another* sickness.... How little effort it would be, with such vast wealth ... to send me two hundred franks. She has plenty to keep those cowled whoremongers, those low-lived wretches—you know whom I mean....

"But it's her own fault, if she prefers to keep that *pretty* fellow rather than a grave and serious man. ... Good bye, my dear Battus ... who is the *dearest* of all men to me...."[26] Erasmus is full of confused jealousy and contempt, almost afraid not only to lose his female maecenas, but also his dearest of all friends, Battus. In the end he hates Battus and charges him with betrayal.

Later on, when he spent some time in Italy with his publisher, Aldus Manutius, he was housed with his host's father-in-law. He shared the bed with the same Hieronymous Aleander whom he later--in a fit of "abnormal," (homosexual) jealousy—betrayed "because of his Jewish nose."

Additional confused homosexual evidence may be found in Erasmus' correspondence with Servetus. At first there were a number of very warm letters; then he cooled off. And as if to "rub it in" he mentions his own servant, secretary, and body-guard, John Smith, in the most endearing terms. To Ammonius he describes him in glowing terms as "that excellent youth" and elicits similar comments from his friends regarding this young man.

There can be no doubt that Erasmus was an anti-feminist and hence—according to our neurasthenic and psychasthenic findings—incapable of quite "normal" sexual happenings or relations. His entire sexuality is in question. This leads us to the core of our anatomy of the genetic aspect of Erasmus' antisemitism. Certainly, a person is not born antisemitic. But he could be born into an antisemitic atmosphere. Psychological studies have shown that antisemitism is generally the product in a child of a home-environment in which father and mother were constantly at odds. And in many cases, the lack of warmth and love, the constant parental quarrels, mutual beatings, desertion and divorce actions violated conventional standards. Erasmus was the victim of at least some of these unfortunate deprivations, including the early death of his profesionally respectable father. They marked the life of Desiderius, and the resulting weaknesses of character were reactivated under the tutelage of the Brethren of the Common Life.

Do we have any evidence that Erasmus tried to combat his predisposition to antisemitism to minimize his anxieties? Our psycho-analytical guides answer that "where anti-semitism is demonstrated in the patient's cultural environment, individuals with this specific syndrome will utilize this handy prejudice for their own irrational prejudices." W. Welzig, the commentator of Erasmus' works, referring to the Rotterdamer's *Ratio* and its antisemitic excesses, said in a footnote: "When Erasmus sometimes grew polemical, he could be wholly tendentious, so that he ceased to be aware of the silliness of his exaggeration."

Antisemites are deprived and lonely people, living as it were as the fringe of society, unless they can make their talents and their neurosis useful to a movement. Their needs are abounding, unsatiable, involving violence and hatred. They crave the things they do not possess. This was also true of Erasmus. This is why he always alluded to Jewish wealth and monetary corruption (they were, allegedly, with their shekels behind the Reformation struggle). His sycophancy may be a side-aspect of this tendency. But basically he rejected himself by envying others. The result was an attempt to find and to erect defense mechanisms. Antisemitism was one, as it represented an effort to displace the self-destroying trends in a personality. As Ackerman and Jahoda pointed out in summary: "At the psychic level, anti-Semitic hostility can be viewed as a profound, though irrational and futile, defensive effort to restore a crippled self. At the social level, it can be regarded as a device for achieving secondary emotional and material gain."

In our earlier observations it was indicated that paternal deprivation in childhood became manifest as the child approached and worked through the Oedipus conflict. This conflict had a profound impact on a young man concerning the image he had of his father, or a political or religious authority. George R. Back has shown for instance that father-deprived children produce an idealistic father image in their fantasy that reveals a secret longing for paternal affection. If, as in the case of Erasmus, the father was gone—by death or divorce, his image tended to become idealized. Peter Lowenberg called it a "reaction formation" or in the vernacular: a defense against a hatred toward the father by replacing these hostile, repressed feelings with their conscious opposite.[27] Such a paternal absence may result in an ever increasing closeness to the mother. This in turn, so Freudian psychologists tell us, will heighten the Oedipal conflict for the son in latency. And during this period a marked increase in the strength of the defenses against sexual drives are noticeable. The beneficial aspects of this situation are that children who experience this deprivation are in a good position to develop intellectually and otherwise express calmness and learn well. The child thus achieves the tools with which to counter sexual desires at puberty. This fits in perfectly well with our picture of Erasmus. For he indeed lost his father at the age of fourteen, left home and was moved to an intellectual environment in which he matured fast, mentally and sexually, although his sexuality moved in a peculiar direction. And since Erasmus had misgivings about his incestuous past, his growing toward puberty stimulated, unhappily for him, incestuous fantasies, and increased his fears of punishment for these forbidden longings.

In the beginning of this chapter we alluded to Erasmus' clinical picture. With his psychasthenic condition, is it small wonder then that his anxieties also involved his fear of being castrated, forcing the lonely boy (with or without his mother) to identify with his "absent" idealized father and perhaps even resulted in having homosexual longings for him? Stated Peter Lowenberg: "The homosexual feelings for the distant father are a love for him shared with the mother and a defense against heightened incestuous feelings for her."

There are perhaps one or two more avenues open to us to explore the strange behavior of Erasmus. Could it possibly be that he at any one given time identified himself with The Christ? Or, did he at any one moment regard himself as the Christ? As far fetched as it may seem, some modern psychologists did come across certain clinical observations that bring this issue within the realm of possibilities. Milton Rokeach in his book *The Three Christs of Ypsilanti* studies three types of men who identified with Christ, who had the delusion of being Christ. Could it possibly be that Erasmus had such delusions?

Rokeach believed that his three clinical cases discarded their original identities and "suffered from paranoid delusions of grandeur, not as a defense against homosexuality but as a defense against confusion about sexual identity. If a person is confused about his sexual identity, he will indeed in certain instances manifest homosexuality. But, in these instances, homosexuality is actually part of a broader picture of confusion about sexual identity." We cannot possibly pin down Erasmus' role as The Christ of his time or his "play-acting" in that role. However, of what Rokeach calls the paranoid delusions of grandeur, these manifestations are ample. Erasmus did regard himself as The Man of his Time and he brooked no competitor. Yet, we do know that his monastic upbringing had somehow conditioned him to be "against" it. Despite the two papal dispensations to throw off his clerical garb and to be released from his vows, he—unlike the Monk Luther, who married an ex-nun—never became involved with the opposite sex. If he had, it could have freed him from misgivings and frustrations. As the priest of Isis said to Lucius, "Once you have begun to serve the Goddess, you will all the more enjoy the fruit of your liberation."[28]

As a follower of Christ, as a person who identified with his Savior and his Father, Erasmus could not afford to have a sexual commitment. At best, he remained as ambiguous as he was in everything else. Had he made a decision for "normalcy in sexual relations," it would have been tantamount to a betrayal, of his Father, the Christ. However, the betrayal of men is something different altogether, for they are antagonists. This writer believes that Erasmus perceived of his calling within the context of his personal need to be the Savior of Christianity. One key to this problem lies again in his precarious health. Did it induce the humanist unconscious fantasies, beginning in his childhood and later on in life, aggravated by long periods of loneliness? Are they of any value to us as we try to come to some plausible interpretation? Could it possibly be that this unloved person, fearful of injury and dirt, saw himself in a sublimated role, rejecting physical love and transferring it to a higher plateau, the love for a pure Christ, with him as his secular Deputy? He was like many men in history beset by doubts, due to his own infirmities: Moses refused to be God's spokesman due to his speech defect; yet he became his people's charismatic leader. Jeremia, one of the greatest prophets in the Old Testament, felt himself too simple to undertake God's summons. St. Paul, the epileptic, had to prove himself in the eyes of Jesus' sincere followers. What about Ignatius of Loyola, the sick knight, who became the Church's authentic military and educational arm? History is full of charismatic heroes, who through doubt in their "capacity," despite a melancholic life-style, inability to marry or to respond to human love became creatively potent. Did not all of these heroes suffer, displayed hatred[29] for their fathers (or mother as in Jeremia's case; or in the case of Moses against his Pharao, Egypt's God-Father)? Erasmus, as we read him, saw in his melancholic moments a punishment from God; however, by becoming detached from libidinal ties to women, his emotions were free to love only one source: Christ. This is why Erasmus remained all his life alone, despite his valiant attempts to break out of his spiritual vice; he was a masterful actor in his own time, a narcissist and intellectually independent. Max Weber suggested:

that the holders of charisma often live in celibacy or at least renounce family life and in fact are single as stated in the call to asceticism of Jesus: "If any man come to me and hates not his father, and mother, and wife, and children, and brethren, and sisters, yea, and his own life also, he cannot be my disciple (Luke 14:26).[30]

Hence, Erasmus' self-love almost demanded that he be recognized as western Humanism's charismatic leader. This was indeed a romantic dream. And did he not act out his role to perfection? Did he not in fact become one of his era's foremost fantasy-heroes? Erasmus had to be much more than just a literatus, he had to become a leader of Christian men, a world-improver. Is this then perhaps the reason why he travelled so much to bring his message to the important parts of western Europe? From there to megalomania is just one step: he became humanism's inspired and authentic Christian. Hence his identification with St. Paul, Jerome, Chrysostomus and others. Erasmus was Don Quixote, "a chivalrous Christian."

The Authoritarian Character

In the historic perspective, Humanism can be called the intellectual bridge between two eras: The Middle Ages and the Renaissance. What concerns the psychohistorian is this: What happened to the educated people during this period, how did they react to The New Mood that was developing away from the sinister, the mystic, the ecclesiastical authority that was gradually replaced by the Renaissance? Was there an awareness of the changes? Had the Renaissance man all of a sudden become an alien to his heretofore Christ-centered life? Or did man gradually develop a desire to establish new priorities for his existence so that he could believe in himself and his unlimited potential, but at the same time still believe in the age-old traditions of his Church? Could Humanism create something of a New Authority that was still Christian and at the same time remain anchored in the past?

To be sure, man had an emotional and rational attachment to the past, to the Mother Church. He identified with her. Yet psychoanalysis has shown that only a fraction of man's thought and behavior is rational. And what about the irrational, the unconscious, and the emotions of men, but also of the child in the man?[31] Sigmund Freud pointed out some sixty years ago that children moving toward maturation are plagued by frustrations

Martin Luther as Junker George, ca 1521. In the Weimar Schloss Museum.

which make them relapse into an earlier period. They almost hate growing up. The results are anxiety or unresolved conflicts. Primitive kinds of gratification, including sexual, may become part of the same picture.

It is possible that Erasmus too had feelings of abandonment, that he regressed, that he was traumatized by fears—particularly in the face of his precarious home situation? But beyond that, did not the adult German, conscious of the fact that the old era was dead and a new era dawning, did he not regress also? To which image was he to cling? Was man really capable of coping with these internal and external pressures? It should not confound the historian that man in general, living in that period of change, had to justify his own negative responses to change by identifying a totally alien culture that then might be held responsible for all of his personal or national woes. The Jew for instance could be the alien responsible for everything felt to be alien in the present. Does not man always show inclinations to glorify the distant past and long to return to it? But could Erasmus identify with or go back mentally or physically, to an absent Father, the source of all his strength?

We know from the biography of Erasmus that he could not return to his father. This was his Ego-destroying catastrophe. And it hit him even the harder because as an alert and perceptive youth he knew what bothered him. His letters bear that out as was pointed out above. And he carried this trauma into adulthood. It made him helpless to face up to new situations, and worst of all, it made him irrational. At this critical point, Erasmus' authoritarian personality was born. If one adds to this picture that Erasmus in his early youth was also deprived of the closeness to his mother, does it surprise us then that Erasmus because of this break became withdrawn and that he isolated himself socially? After all, one of his difficulties was, as we have seen, his inability to establish lasting friendships. This absence of love at the bosom of his mother and subsequent loneliness without a circle of real friends, made him rage with frustration and evoke feelings of terror; worst of all, deprivation made him believe that he was a reject due to his being evil, the kind of evil that repels others who sense that something is wrong with that loveless, ego-weakened person.

Erasmus as a consequence became ill since he was unable to shake off his creatureliness or his exaggerated worthlessness. Hannah Arendt in *The Origins of Totalitarianism* speaks of twentieth century man's loneliness as we find it so prevalent in the life of Erasmus, four hundred years before the industrial revolution, imperialism, and the new world of changing moral and political values. "Loneliness, the common ground for terror, the essence of totalitarian government, and for ideology or logicality, the preparation of its executioners and victims, is closely connected with uprootedness and superfluousness. . . . To be uprooted means to have no place in the world, recognized and guaranteed by others; to be superfluous means not to belong to the world at all. . . ."

Again, Erasmus, driven against the ropes, had to break out of this cornered situation and try to get even with those who had created his dilemma. He had to find a scapegoat who had disturbed or injured him, hurt or rejected him. Whether real or not, it did not matter. The Jew met that psychological demand. He became Erasmus' challenger. We are not suggesting that Erasmus and Hitler are synonymous. However, in recent years studies suggest that the Lutheran Reformation had conditioned the German mind, that its authoritarian appeal helped the Führer to project his ideology on a susceptible Father-image, hungry people. Hitler was the new father image for the Germans between two eras, the German Empire of a disgraced Kaiser Wilhelm II, and the New Third Reich. Father Wilhelm was gone and Adolph became his deputy, a *Stellvertreter* in the word's fullest meaning.[32] In his article, "The Unsuccessful Adolescense of H. Himmler,"[33] Peter Loewenberg made the following observations reminiscent also of Erasmus' early youth: "Hitler became a father figure to him. The new religion of National Socialism became his way out of the inner prohibitions presented by father and Church. These he now could give up for a new set of ideals that allowed him to express aggression. His archaic super-ego was still, however, dependent on identification with his environment. He needed to please Hitler. . . . National Socialist ideology offered him a substitute for his Christian super-ego or conscience (*i.e.* The Mother Church. Hitler too was a Catholic!). . . . It gave him a leader to whom he could submit and from whom he received superego sanction to act out his libidinal and aggressive fantasies."

Rolling history back by four hundred years, we have the identical painful situation in Erasmus. We have already seen how and why Jesus became Erasmus' father-figure and substitute. For the rest of his life Erasmus was now free to play out his libidinal aggressions; he could surrender to his utopian fantasies. Jesus had charged him to be His defender of the true Faith. And for this he was willing to assume full responsibilities—even if it meant to combat and to annihilate his enemies, the Jews. As Loewenberg observed: "Adolescence contains an infantile admixture that often causes it to appear bizzare and aberrant. The youth-in-crisis shifts rapidly from melancholic depths of isolation, loneliness and depression to the exhilirated heaven of megalomaniac fantasies."[34] Looking again upon Erasmus, we get the impression that he remained all his life an adolescent, experiencing the most painful depths of emotions and the heights of religious exultation, yet they kept him chained to the loneliness of his existence. It seems that the whole Reformation upheaval, the dogmatic posturing of the old and new Churches, the claims of all reformation personalities (Calvin, Luther, Zwingli—and the Papacy) to infallibility, the initiation of the Fuehrer Principle, all of these things brought about a cultural regression, culminating in years of Religious Wars that all but destroyed the German Lands. The other byproduct was a moral hangover, if not romantic hankering for a Second Renaissance, leading to what is called the Enlightenment. The final Medieval culture-shock came after the defeat of Nazism in our lifetime.

For a fuller understanding of Erasmus, a few more voices ought to be heard. Erich Fromm in discussing the authoritarian character speaks of two sexes: the powerful one and the powerless.[35]

His love, admiration and readiness for submission are automatically aroused by power, whether of a person or of an institution. Power fascinates him not for any values for which a specific power may stand, but just because it is power. Just as his "love" is automatically aroused by power, so powerless people or institutions automatically arouse his contempt. The very sight of a powerless person makes him want to attack, dominate, humiliate

Erasmus of Rotterdam. Lanfield Castle near Salisbury. By Holbein, the Younger.

him. Whereas a different kind of character is appalled by the idea of attacking one who is helpless, the authoritarian character feels the more aroused the more helpless his object has become.

Fromm concludes on this rather optimistic note:

The function of an authoritarian ideology and practice can be compared to the function of neurotic symptoms. Such symptoms result from unbearable psychological conditions and at the same time offer a solution that makes life possible. Yet they are not a solution that leads to happiness or growth of personality. They leave unchanged the conditions that necessitate the neurotic solution. . . . The history of mankind is the history of growing individuation, but it is also the history of growing freedom. The quest for freedom is not a metaphysical force and cannot be explained by natural law; it is the necessary result of the process of individuation and of the growth of culture. The authoritarian systems cannot do away with the basic conditions that make for the quest for freedom; neither can they exterminate the quest for freedom that springs from these conditions."

We may suppose that Erasmus' authoritarian character did indeed perceive in his time this quest for the realization of his potentialities, that he somehow grappled for this thing called inner freedom, but also that he did not succeed in either realm. He remained throughout his life too much the captive of his sick inner self which he was unable to overcome.

None other than Max I. Dimont in his most perceptive book *The Indestructible Jews* made this summary observation:

We can now perceive the underlying unity between chiliastic and totalitarian thought, for the chiliastic mind is closer to that of the modern dictator than to that of the ancient tyrant. Though a tyrant is ruthless, he generally does not kill if he is not opposed in his arbitrary rule; he is mainly concerned with maintaining his own power and the system of privileges it entails. The dictator, on the other hand, kills in the name of an ideology because he conceives of himself as the harbinger of the perfect state. He kills anyone he thinks will not fit the Procrustean[36] blueprint of his state. Those whose ideas extend beyond the blueprint must be chopped down to fit; those who fall short of its ideology must be stretched to size. Thus, in both the chiliastic and totalitarian regimes, people are doomed to death not only for active opposition but for not fitting the framework of an ideology.

The parallels between chiliastic and totalitarian thought can now be brought into sharper focus. In the chiliastic fantasy, the true believers are the self-elected Saints of God; the enemy is the forces of anti-Christ which, if exterminated, would usher in the Christian paradise. In the communist fantasy, the true believers are the self-elected members of the proletariat; the enemy is the capitalist class, whose elimination would herald the arrival of the bolshevik paradise. In the Nazi fantasy, the true believers are the self-elected members of the German race; the enemy is the Jewish people, whose destruction would signal the start of the Aryan paradise.[37]

There is an air of unrealism about it all. And it makes one shudder that Erasmus' dream was not so far removed from the dream the Germans entertained in our own lifetime. This unreal dream turned into a nightmare for those who witnessed the acting-out. Erasmus' life too turned into a nightmare, for him and for those who can see him today for what he really was: a totalitarian, willing to be both master and slave. In being so, he destroyed for himself the world of Humanism, and he has destroyed for us modern historians, the belief that he was indeed The Prince of Humanism.

NOTES

[1] B. W. T. Nuyens, *Geschiedenis der Geneeskunde* (Leiden, 1936), p. 80.
[2] A. Werthemann. *Schaedel und Gebeine des Erasmus von Rotterdam* (Hague, 1930).
[3] V. W. D. Schenk, *Erasmus' Character and Deseases* (Leiden, 1947), p. 91.
[4] *Ibid.*, p. 8.
[5] "Ex *illicito* et ut timet *incesto damnatoque* coitu."
[6] R. Friedenthal, *Luther* (Munich, 1967), p. 312.
[7] *Desiderius Erasmus* (New York, 1899), p. 48.
[8] Benjamin B. Wolman, *The Psychoanalytic Interpretation of History* (New York, 1971), p. 107.
[9] W. T. H. Jackson, *Essential Works of Erasmus* (New York, 1965), p. 19.
[10] *Life, Character and Influence of Desiderius Erasmus of Rotterdam* (New York, 1928), p. N 16.
[11] *Ibid.*, p. VIII.
[12] Erasmus Desiderius, *The Praise of Folly*, translated by H. H. Hudson, p. 85.
[13] Droyden asks this question: "Is Erasmus' lack of objectivity a lifeless academic affair, something he denounced as "eunuchic"?
[14] Wolman, p. 41.
[15] *Ibid.*, p. 99.
[16] Wilhelm Heitmueller's *Hellenistic Christianity Before Paul* (Goettingen, 1903), made an effort to clarify these theological differences: "It is further to be noted (1) that, so far as I know, in the genuine Jewish literature the Messiah is never called "Lord," so that Jewish believers would not find this a natural way of naming Jesus as the Messiah; (2) that for the Jews the name "Lord" was the specific designation for God himself. On pure Jewish soil, therefore, the prerequisites for origin of the title "Lord" for Jesus were not present. All that leads to the presumption that this designation, so pregnant with consequences, must not have arisen in the primitive church. There remains then only our Hellenistic Christianity. Here the prerequisites for the development of the Messiah Jesus into the "Lord" Jesus Christ were present: the message of the Messiah Jesus, dead, exalted, imminently to come, and the fact that the name "Lord" in pagan circles was a common designation for the diety from whom one expected salvation and whose fate—that was true of some few—in violent death and in exaltation reminded one of the fate of the Messiah Jesus. Here now, at least on pagan soil, the floodgates were opened for Hellenistic-Oriental elements. The proclamation of the death and resurrection of Jesus Christ is not a product of the myth of the dying and "rising" God; nevertheless, when it reached Hellenistic soil it could and must immediately enter in pagan minds into an amalgamation with similar-sounding stories of the violent death and exaltation of gods.

By this name "Lord" Jesus was *ipso facto* given a divine status. With that step was linked unavoidably the cultus, divine worship in some, even if only germinal, form. Though we undoubtedly perceive in Paul the beginnings of

156   The Tragedy of Erasmus

the Christ-cult, still we know now that at this point also he was not the creator but the recipient. He had to accommodate himself to what was given; perhaps he even attenuated what was there."

[17] A timely analogy would be Polish behavior during the seige of the Warsaw Ghetto and after the Jews had been deported to labor camps. Or in Soviet Russia today.

[18] In his *Letters of Obscure Men.*

[19] Poliakov, *The History of Antisemitism* (New York, 1965), pp. 215, 226.

[20] *Les Juifs parmi les nations* (Paris, 1938), p. 21.

[21] J. D. Sutherland, "Gandhi, A Psychoanalytic View," *The American Historical Review* (1971), Vol. 76, No. 4.

[22] Quoted by E. Emerton, *Desiderius Erasmus* (New York, 1899), pp. 50-56.

[23] In *Anti-Semitism and Emotional Disorder*, p. 31.

[24] Only one tract deals with the opposite sex: *The Comparation of a Virgin and a Martyr.* As to the Marian Cult: it is the adoration of the divine motherhood, virginity, immaculate conception and assumption of Mary, the mother of Jesus. It dates back to the second century. Francisco Suarez (d. 1617) is regarded the father of scientific Mariology.

[25] In *Desiderius Erasmus of Rotterdam.*

[26] In a further letter he reduced the ante to one hundred franks!

[27] Peter Lowenberg, "The Psychohistorical Origins of the Nazi Youth Cohorts," *The American Historical Review* (1971), Vol. 76, # 5, pp. 1485-86.

[28] Ovid, *Metamorphoses* XI, 15; quoted in M. Dibelius' *Paul, Mystic and Prophet* (Berlin, 1970), p. 403.

[29] Hatred is the ultimate form of resentment.

[30] *Essays in Sociology*, "The Sociology of Charismatic Authority" (New York, 1958), pp. 245-8.

[31] Lowenberg, p. 1461.

[32] Literally: to stand in his place.

[33] Peter Lowenberg in the "Unsuccessful Adolescence of H. Himmler," *The American Historical Review*, Vol. 76, #3, pp. 637 ff.

[34] *Ibid.*, pp. 639-641.

[35] *Escape from Freedom* (London, 1942). This chapter was taken from Gilbert Allardyce, *The Place of Fascism in European History* (Englewood Cliffs, N. J.), p. 43 ff.

[36] In Greek mythology, Procrustes was an innkeeper who had a bed which any lodger using it had to fit. If the traveler was too tall, his legs were sawed off to the proper length; if too short, he was stretched on a rack to fit it.

[37] Max I. Dimont, *The Indestructible Jews* (New York, 1971), pp. 377-378.

9

Humanism Reconsidered

The starting point of the Humanistic era was the late Middle Ages. The men of the New Mood were trying to promote for educational purposes the study of the classics in a rational, if not secular, manner. Since this new education was not oriented to the Church and not dominated by the Catholic hierarchy, it held promise for society. It was meant to set man free from tradition. Beyond that, it started to postulate a new goal, heretofore ignored, namely to strive for the betterment of the individual and of all mankind. In the Middle Ages, the Church's earthy goal was to achieve the individual's salvation for the good life to come. During the period we associate with Humanism, man became earth-centered and aware not only of his own urgent needs for intellectual expansion but also for the growth of the society in which he lived. National and international concerns grew out of this new posture. Hence, man no longer could ideally afford the luxuries of intellectual, traditional intolerance or religious discrimination against any person or any people.[1]

That the Humanist spirit in northwestern Europe remained more deeply anchored in the medieval Christian tradition can be understood for several reasons: Historically speaking these mostly Germanic lands had still a missionary orientation due to the relatively late arrival of a well-organized Church. Italy by contrast was a Bastion, the Rock of the monolithic Organization, the Western Church. Secondly, with the advance of the Turks, Italy had been swamped at the time of the Renaissance with Ebionist, anti-Trinitarians, Eastern Mediterranean artisans and artists, and by Greek and Hellenistic scholars. Germany on the other hand did not at first have the opportunity to face up to this liberalizing and liberating influence. It remained pietistic, "corresponding to the deeper Teutonic semi-Protestant spirit." Erasmus was temperamentally not attuned to the lighthearted, if not irreverent, Italians. Antiquity was used by him not to brighten but as an educational vehicle, a moral device to make man return to better Christian living. It was reactionary, in that it was not really freeing man from his traditional fetters. Italian Humanism smiled, Erasmian Humanism frowned. To Erasmus, non-German Humanism was amoral; his own kind was moral for the good of a new Humanitas Christiana (with the accent on the latter word). That Erasmus could not think in broader terms, was not really his fault.[2] And it is idle to speculate what could have happened if he had arrived at a more universal application of Humanism, or had he been born or lived in Italy for the major part of his life. Being a child of Monasticism, little more could have been expected of him, unless, had he been under the guidance of a more "enlightened" man, such as Pico. Today our definition of Humanism would be more all-embracing. It would certainly not be regional or sectarian. In the words of Osborn: "Morality and Universality ... go together. The truly moral man, the good man, regards himself as obligated to *all* men, not some men only; he strives to think in terms of humanity; his notion of society embraces, at least in principle, all men."[3] J. A. Mazzeo made a valid observation when he said that Erasmus preferred to emulate the ancients, rather than to imitate them. This bears out what we have been trying to convey: The Italian Humanists gloried in reviving the mode of living of the ancient Greeks which led them toward a freer, more nonconformist living, quite unlike the Erasmian ideal. As M. M. Phillips has pointed out, "The intoxicated celebration of human potentials, which gave its glitter to the Italian Renaissance, was foreign to his mind."[4] We see throughout Erasmus' work a conformism to models: to Christ, Socrates, and others. Here again, Italy and Germany were and still are temperamentally opposites, but Erasmus was unaware of this cultural burden. "That he did not adapt himself to the changing scene, seems to have been Erasmus' mistake."

It is perhaps heresy to call Erasmus an anti-intellectual unless one considers that he had a deep distrust of the human spirit or the powers of the intellect. Despite Erasmus' educational program, he proved in the last analysis that he was indeed not an intellectual by our modern definition. His own words indicted him: "The goal of all learning is the Good Life." We have to understand what he meant by that. To him the Good Life had nothing to to with what the Italians called virtu. Erasmus had the good Christian life in mind. And that did not have to be necessarily based on an intellectual foundation. It had the ring of exclusivism and medievalism. After all, he never identified himself with the term Christian Renaissance. He spoke constantly about the "Restitutio Christianismi," a restoration of Christianity. It was a religious program of the kind Mohammed Iqbal envisioned for Indian Moslems in our century. Neither man was "great"; at best they were synthesizers and amalgamators between religion and some kind of a naturalistic ethic. Heinrich Weinstock, in his book *Die Tragoedie des Humanismus* asked a relevant question: So what does his humanitas look like? But, if Erasmus in his own imperturbable self-confidence is not only unChristian, but even irreligious in general—how can he be then possibly humane, when humanitas really implies the total, true reality of a human being?[5] A few pages later on, he gives this answer: "In other words: the only true and possible humanism and the kind that has the possibility of self-realization is the one which is tragic or has broken the Christian way asunder because this is the sole, real Humanism. However, the unbroken and unconditional kind of Erasmus must be regarded as illusionary or mongrellized. It must either comfort or destroy. . . . It is therefore basically non-or antihumanistic. . . . It is a sterile makeshift."

Weinstock sees in Erasmus' style of Humanism a built-in, self-destructive force, which contributed in destroying him. It was Erasmus' basic pessimism, which restricted him from the Humanist Garden. The *Theatrum Mundi* became a Tragoedia Mundi, and Erasmus its none too heroic actor. Bientenholz expressed it in more pragmatic terms: "In view of his basically doubtful attitude toward human progress, the blissful expectation of a Golden Age seems rather illogical."[6] What made Erasmus' Humanism even more restrictive is that he tried to fasten it to his religious medievalism. He did not understand the implications of European expansionism or internationalism, economic, cultural, and political. His *res publica Christiana* was of another world. As with so many other humanists, Erasmus' world is a dream, and the attempt to build a bridge between those two radically different worlds, made his utopia unworkable. In the words of B. F. Skinner "the most important feature of the utopian design is that the survival of a community can be made important only to its members."[7] In the absence of enforceable laws and agencies, utopian societies remain at best voluntary fraternities of a few loosely knit absentee personalities who may or may not wish to have a closer contact than occasional meetings or exchange intellectual letters or pamphlets. Indeed, Utopia means unworkability. Mass-man is excluded. In Utopia time stands still. History is suspended. Erasmus' religious humanism was anachronistic. He addressed himself to the masses he despised, and wrote for a Christian nobility in a spirit which was neither truly Christian nor noble. He spoke and wrote to himself. He was a monologist writing frantic messages and verbose treatises to a handful of fellow Humanists, encouraging one or hating another in a mood of unrealism and quixotic impism. This was the real Humanist tragedia Erasmiana. To sum it up: "Humanism was for the happy few, not for the broad multitude, it was never anything better than a kingdom set amid the clouds lighting up for a moment the whole world, beautiful to contemplate, a pure picture painted by a creative mind, looking down serenely from its unattainable heights upon the tenebrous world below. Such an airy and artificial structure could make no stand against a genuine storm. It was doomed to perish unresistingly, and to fall into oblivion."

An air of uncertainty pervades much of Erasmus' writings, and the underlying Humanist's struggle with God and history, faith and reason, remained unresolved until Humanists lodged either in the camp of the Reformation with a demanding but more tangible Faith, or as in the world of the Kabbala—the never-never land of divine speculation, or as in the Enlightenment, which relegated

Christianity to a position of secondary importance. What Erasmus did not see or find was that in a more enlightened Christian climate, man wished to establish priorities for living and to move toward a more understanding, intellectual Christian virtue. Erasmian Humanism had a musty, all-pervasive odor of pessimism, a reflection of his own personal unhappy disposition, which kept him in monastic chains all of his life—despite a meandering urge to escape his intellectual confinements. T. G. Masaryk observed: "Pessimism is not only contemporaneous with utilitarianism, but is also related in its goals. Utilitarianism affirms that each individual pursues his own happiness, his pleasures, and only his pleasures. Pessimism likewise pursued happiness, but it reaches the conclusion that happiness is not accessible." [8]

Gottfried W. Locher sees Erasmus' legacy in a different light. "He is the Christian witness of humanity for the modern times . . . and he has anchored humanism deeply in the metaphysical. With his Philosophia Christiana he was able to extend the dialogue between Christians and non-Christians to broader common themes. . . . He has . . . impressed unto our consciences tasks that are not yet fulfilled and born upon our souls: world-peace, the unity of truth and freedom, the humanity of human beings." [9] This sounds more like Professor Locher's hopes for the future than anything Erasmus ever envisioned in his own life. Erasmus of all the humanists had no intention of involving non-Chistians or Jews with his Christ-centered philosophy. For that he was too morose and prejudiced. The World Peace he advocated was racist in nature, it was a *Pax Christiana et Excludans* closed to "heretics," Moors and Jews alike. It was the Christian Humanist Ghetto behind whose walls Christians might talk to each other—as long as it was on Erasmus' terms. The humanitas Erasmus fought for was a mixture of pietism, Greek-style sophistry, and Germanic arrogance, metaphysical unrealism and educational innovations. Even viewed from a sixteenth century watchtower, Erasmus was a petty knight, nongenerous and vengeful, theoretically full of compassion for "his own kind of people," [10] but unwilling to search and to find the humaneness in men.

Erasmus was a man who taught the world "how to live in peace but who ultimately saw all his admonitions disregarded, his hopes dashed, his ideas shattered by greedy, rapacious, and stupid men."[11] This is reading too much into Erasmus' work. We must ask the decisive question: How can a man who was never at peace with himself, who had a christological obsession, who was a fanatic á la Savonarola, how could he have hoped for a world at peace while fighting for his own disorganized potpourri of theological, utopian humanism? Erasmus was not a man of peace. He was—as some of his contemporaries called him in an irreverent mood of derision—an "Erasinus," an erring ass. We recognize his efforts to bring a variety of "modern" ideas into late medieval thought patterns; and we admire his independence which was risky as he danced with virtuosity between the Inquisitors and the Reformers. "It is not an unfair criticism to say that his conceptions of man, society, and the state, admirable as they are in their burning idealism, often seem lifeless because, while they have much esprit, they lack body. Or to put it differently, his good wine spills because he provides no receptacle for it." With his almost photographic mind he poured out prolific writings, all lacking in depth. Humanists were only qualifiedly modernists. We have to understand the limitations of that humanist world. They were dabblers in all those things that had been tabooed by the Church. Only the Christian Kabbalists constituted a separate breed of men: they tried to go into the depth of human existence. They at least made a devout effort to understand themselves by speculating about God and His hosts. Erasmus was foreign to this world, and all he did was a kind of tinkering with the Absolute—just as he tinkered with everything else. The measure of his greatness was not his vast literary outpourings. His full measure was the depth which he tried to penetrate, but failed due to his unfortunate temperament. It was reserved to a man of Maritains's stature to state ideally what the true Christian humanist position ought to be: "For the Christian the true religion is essentially supernatural and, because it is supernatural, it is not a part of man nor of the world, nor of a race, nor of a culture, nor of civilization; it is strictly universal."[12] At this point modern Christianity and Judaism have arrived at a common ground. Unfortunately for Erasmus, his time and he himself were not ready for such a declaration of Faith.

Erasmus was a man full of inner contradiction, a tragic person, who perhaps could not help being the way he was. And so, when we discuss his humanism, his religious philosophy, his political and economic views, his obsession with the Jewish Question, all of these problems are part and parcel of the total picture of Erasmus. We are writing this post mortem not because we "hate" him, but because we have a deeply felt sense of compassion with his illnesses and paradoxical behavior. If the spotlight fell on him unsparingly, then it was only to debunk those men and ideas who for too long have seen this humanist under the rosy cloud of their own day-dreaming experience. To the historians who read these lines we say that we do not share Hegel's pessimistic view that history teaches us that man learns nothing from history.

NOTES

[1] Corliss Lamont, *The Philosophy of Humanism* (London, 1957).
[2] F. Caspari makes another point, again pinpointing Erasmus' ambiguity: "... There are too many contradictions between the worlds of classical antiquity and Christianity that Erasmus chooses to gloss over rather than to reconcile." And may we add here that behind it all is the basic conflict between Faith and Reason which has plagued all men of faith and which has not been resolved even in our time. "Erasmus on Social Functions of Humanism," in *Journal of the History of Ideas*, #8, 1947, p. 89ff.
[3] R. Osborn, *Humanism and Moral Theory* (London, 1959), pp. 67-68.
[4] M. M. Phillips, *Erasmus and the Northern Renaissance* (Cambridge, 1964), p. XXIV.
[5] *Ibid.*, p. 197. "Wie steht es dann mit seiner Humanitas? Aber wenn Erasmus in seinem unerschütterlichen Selbstvertrauen *nicht nur unchristlich, sondern unreligiös uberhaupt* ist - wie kann er dann sein, wenn anders Humanitas die ganze wahre Wirklichkeit des Menschen meint?" (Original German Quote)
[6] Peter G. Bientenholz, *Humanism and Biography in the Works of Erasmus of Rotterdam* (Geneva, 1966), p. 31.
[7] B. F. Skinner, *Beyond Freedom and Dignity* (New York, 1971), pp. 153-156.
[8] T. G. Masaryk, *Humanistic Ideals* (London, 1956), p. 9.
[9] *Zwingli and Erasmus*, p. 60.
[10] "... not very deeply committed," A. N. Marlow and B. Drewery, *Luther and Erasmus, Free Will and Salvation* (New York, 1970).
[11] F. Caspari, "Erasmus and the Social Functions of Christian Humanism," in *Journal of the History of Ideas*, #8, 1947.
[12] Jacques Maritain, *True Humanism* (New York, 1954), pp. 89-90.

SUGGESTED READINGS

Ackerman, Nathan W. and Marie Jahoda, *Anti-Semitism and Emotional Disorder* (New York, 1950).
Aldridge, John William, *The Hermeneutic of Erasmus* (John Knox Press, 1966).
Allen, J. H., *Hebrew Men & Times* (Boston, 1883).
Allen, P. S., *Opus Epistolarum Des. Erasmi Roterodami,* Vol. 1-11 (Oxford, 1906-47).
―――――, "Erasmus, Lectures and Wayfaring Sketches," in *The Three Lingual Colleges of the Early Sixteenth Century* (Oxford, 1934).
―――――, *The Age of Erasmus* (London, 1963).
Arendt, Hannah, *The Origins of Totalitarianism* (New York, 1966).
Atkinson, James, *M. Luther and the Birth of Protestantism* (Baltimore, 1968).
Bainton, Roland H., *Erasmus of Christendom* (New York, 1969).
Baldwin, M. W., *Christianity Through the 13th Century* (New York, 1970).
Bientenholz, Peter G., *History and Biography in the Work of Erasmus of Rotterdam* (Geneva, 1966).
Blau, Joseph Leon, *The Christian Interpretation of the Cabala in the Renaissance* (New York, 1944).
Bondurant, Joan V., Margaret W. Fisher, and J. D. Sutherland, *Gandhi, A Psychoanalytic View* (*The American Historic Review,* 76, # 4).
Brod, Max, *Johannes Reuchlin und sein Kampf* (Stuttgart, 1965).
Bronowski, Jacob and Bruce Mazlish, "Man Out of Season," (*Horizon,* 4 No. 5., St. Marian, Ohio, May, 1962).
Caspari, Fritz. "Erasmus on the Social Functions of Christian Humanism" (*Journal of the History of Ideas,* 8, 1947).
Cole, H. N., "Erasmus and His Diseases" (*Journal of American Medical Association,* 148, No. 7, July, 1952).
Dickens, A. G., *Martin Luther and the Reformation* (New York, 1967).
Dimont, Max I., *The Indestructable Jews* (New York, 1971).
Dolan, John P., *The Essential Erasmus* (New York, 1967).
Dresden, Samuel, *Humanism in the Renaissance* (Munich, 1968).

168   The Tragedy of Erasmus

Eckert, Willehad Paul, *Erasmus Von Rotterdam* (Werk and Wirkung I, Köln, 1967).
_____ , *Erasmus Von Rotterdam* (Werk and Wirkung II, Köln, 1967).
_____ , "Hoch and Spaet Mittelater - Katholischer Humanismus" *(Kirche and Synagogue, Handbuch von Christen und Juden,* Stuttgart, 1968).
Elton, G. R., *Reformation Europe* (New York, 1963).
Emerton, Ephraim, *Desiderius Erasmus of Rotterdam* (New York, 1896).
Erasmus, Desiderius, *The Praise of Folly* (Yale, 1947, translated by H. H. Hudson).
_____ , *Inquisitio De Fide* (Yale University Press, 1950, translated by C. R. Thompson).
_____ , *Christian Humanism and the Reformation* (New York, 1969, Ed. by J. C. Olin).
_____ , *Discourse on Free Will* (New York, 1965, edited by E. F. Winter).
_____ , *The Immense Mercy of God* (California State Library, 1940, Intro. by E. M. Hulme).
_____ , *Handbook of the Militant Christian* (Notre Dame, 1967).
_____ , *The Education of a Christian Prince* (New York 1965, translated by L. K. Born).
_____ , *On Copia of Words and Ideas* (Marquette University Press, 1948, translated by D. B. King; H. D. Rix).
Erasmus von Rotterdam, *Faunus and the Epicure* (University of Chicago Press, 1969, translated by Gerrard; Edited by R. A. Allen).
_____ , *Ausgewaehlte Schriften III* (Darmstadt, 1967, edited and translated by Werner Welzig).
Erasmus von Rotterdam, *Ausgewaehlte Schriften II* (Wissenschaftliche Buchgesellschaft, Darmstadt, 1969, W. Welzig.
_____ , *Colloquia Familiaria* (Darmstadt, 1968, translated by Werner Welzig).
_____ , "Epistola ad Paulum Volzium," *Enchiridion Militis Christiana* (Translated by Werner Welzig, Darmstadt, 1968).
Erickson, Eric, *The Young Man Luther* (New York, 1958).
Faulkner, John Alfred, *Erasmus: The Scholar* (New York, 1907).
Ferguson, W. K., *Renaissance Studies* (University of West Ontario, London, 1963).
Fischer, David Hackett, *Historians' Fallacies* (New York, 1970).
Friedenthal, Richard, *Luther, Sein Leben and Seine Zeit* (Munich, 1967 and 1971).
Fromm, Erich, *Escape from Freedom* (London, 1942).

Suggested Readings 169

Geiger, Ludwig, *J. Reuchlin, Sein Leben und Sein Werk* (Leipzig, 1871).
───── , *Renaissance in Humanism in Germany and Italy* (Berlin, 1882).
Gelder, Enno van, H. A., *The Two Reformations in the Sixteenth Century* (The Hague, 1961).
Gilmore, Myron P. *Humanists and Jurists* (Harvard University Press, 1963).
───── , *The World of Humanism, 1453-1517* (New York, 1952).
Glock, Charles Y. and Rodney Stark, *Christian Beliefs and Anti-Semitism* (New York, 1966).
Graetz, Heinrich, *History of the Jews* (Vol. IV, Philadelphia, 1941).
Gundersheimer, Werner L., *French Humanism, 1470-1600* (New York, 1969).
Hay, Malcolm, *Europe and the Jews* (Boston, 1969).
Heer, Friedrich, *The Medieval World* (New York, 1969).
Hillerbrand, Hans J., *Men and Ideas in the 16th Century* (Chicago, 1968).
Hillerbrand, Hans J., *The Reformation* (New York, 1964).
Howard, Richard, *The History of Anti-Semitism* (New York, 1965).
Huizinga, Johan, *Erasmus and the Age of Reformation* (New York, 1957).
Hyma, Albert, *The Youth of Erasmus* (University of Michigan Press, 1930).
───── , *Erasmus and the Humanists* (New York, 1930).
Jackson, W.T.H., *Essential Works of Erasmus* (New York, 1960).
Kisch, Guido, *Erasmus und die Jurisprudenz seiner Zeit* (Basel, 1960).
───── , "Erasmus Stellung zu Juden and Judentum" (*Philosophie und Geschichte*, Tuebingen, 1969).
Koerber, Eberhard von, *Die Staatheorie des Erasmus von Rotterdam* (Berlin, 1967).
Krebs, Manfred, *Reuchlin's Beziehungen zu Erasmus von Rotterdam* (Pforzheim, 1955).
Kristeller, Paul Oscar, *Renaissance Thought II* (New York, 1967).
Lamont, Corliss, *The Philosophy of Humanism* (New York, 1957).
Laswell, H. D., *The Analysis of Political Behavior* (Hamden, Conn., 1966).
Levi, Albert William, *Humanism and Politics* (Bloomington, Indiana, University Press, 1969).
Levinger, Lee J., *Anti-Semitism Yesterday and Tomorrow* (New York, 1936).

Loewenberg, Peter, "The Psychohistoric Origins of the Nazi Youth" *(The American Historical Review* 76, No. 5, 1971).
───── "The Unsuccessful Adolescence of H. Himmler" *(American Historical Review,* Vol. 76, #3, June, 1971).
Loewenstein, Rudolph M. *Christians and Jews* (International Universities Press, Inc., 1952).
Major, Russell J., *The Age of the Renaissance and Reformation* (Philadelphia, 1970).
Mangan, John Joseph, *Life, Character and Influence of Desiderius Erasmus of Rotterdam* (London, 1928).
Maritain, Jacques, *True Humanism* (New York, 1954).
Mazzeo, Joseph Anthony, *Renaissance and Revolution* (New York, 1965).
Meeks, Wayne A., *The Writings of St. Paul* (New York, 1972).
Murray, Robert H., *Erasmus and Luther* (London, 1920).
Nichols, Francis Morgan, *The Epistles of Erasmus* (New York, 1962).
Nuyens, B.W.T., "Geschiedenes der Geneeskunds" *(Nederland. tijdchrift v. Geneesk,* 80:3157, 1936).
Olin, J. C., *Desiderius Erasmus, Christian Humanism and The Reformation* (New York, 1965).
Payne, John B., *Erasmus, His Theology of the Sacraments* (New York, 1970).
Pascal, Paul, *The Julius Exclusus of Erasmus* (Indiana University Press, 1959).
Pirenne, Henri, *Histoire economique et sociale du Moyen age* (Paris, 1969).
Poliakov, L., *The History of Anti-Semitism* (New York, 1965).
Reynolds, Ernest Edwin, *Thomas Moore and Erasmus* (Fordham University Press, 1965).
Rokeach, Milton, *The Three Christs of Ypsilanti* (New York, 1965).
Rupp, Gordon E., *Luther and Erasmus: Free Will and Salvation* (Philadelphia, 1969).
Schenk, V.W.D., "Erasmus Character and Disease" *(Nederland. tijdschrift v. geneesk,* 91, 1947).
Seebohm, Frederic, *The Oxford Reformers: John Colet, Erasmus, and Thomas More* (London, 1896).
Seigel, Jerrold E., *Rhetoric and Philosophy in Renaissance Humanism* (Princeton University Press, 1968).
Skinner, B. F., *Beyond Freedom and Dignity* (New York, 1971).
Smith, Preserved, *Erasmus: A Study of His Life, Ideals and Place in History* (New York, 1969).
Spitz, Lewis Williams, *The Religious Renaissance of the German Humanists* (Harvard University Press, 1963).

Stone, I. F., *The Passions of the Mind* (New York, 1972).
Taylor, Henry Osborn, *Thought and Expression in the Sixteenth Century* (New York, 1920).
Thompson, Craig R., *The Colloquies of Erasmus* (Chicago, 1965).
⸻ , *Inquisitio de Fide* (Yale Studies # IV. 1967).
Thomson, D.F.S., *Erasmus and Cambridge* (University of Toronto Press, 1970).
Welzig, Werner, *Erasmus' Werke* (Darmstadt, 1967).
Weinstock, Heinrich, *Die Tragöedie des Humanismus* (Berlin, 1956).
Werthemann, A., "Schaedel und Gebeine des Erasmus von Rotterdam" *(Verhandlungen der Naturforsch.* Gesellschaft, 40, 1930).
Winckler, Gerhard B., *Erasmus' Ausgewaehtle Schriften* (in *Wissenschaftliche Buchgesellschaft,* Vol. 1, 1970).
Wolman, Benjamin B., *The Psychoanalytic Interpretation of History* (New York, 1971).

INDEX OF NAMES

Ackerman, Nathan W.
   140, 143
Adrianus, Matthaeus 115,
   116
Agricola, R. 109
Akiba, Rabbi 131
Albert von Brandenburg
   77, 110
Alcala, University of 10,
   110, 111
Aldington of Kent 7
Aldridge, J. W. 95, 96, 97
Alemanno, Johan 119
Aleander, Hieronymous
   46, 48, 141
Alexander VI, Pope 59
Allen, P. S. 35
Amerbach, John 8, 115
Ammonius, Andreas 46,
   141
Anrich 112
Arendt, Hannah 149
Augustine, St. 115

Back, George R. 143
Banisius, Jacob 68, 70
Bartolini 36
Battus, Rhenanus 4, 8,
   128, 140, 141
Bené, Charles 114
Ber, L. 8
Bergen, Henry of 4
Beumer, J., S. J. 110, 111
Bietenholz, Peter 159
Blount, Edward 5
Boerio, Baptiste 6
Bombasius 6
Borsselen, Anne Veere
   Lady of 4, 128, 140,
   141

173

Brant, Sebastian 136
Brod, Max 72, 77, 78, 114
Bronowski, J. 100
Bruno, Giordano 131
Buber, Martin 120
Budé, Guillaume 59
Busche, H. von 64
Busleiden, Hieronymous
    8, 111

Caesarius, John 70, 96
Capito, Wolfgang (Fabricius)
    35, 36, 112, 115
Capnio (Reuchlin) 50
Carondilet, Bishop of
    Byzanz 76
Cateromachus 6
Charcot, Jean-Martin 27
Charles VIII of France
    119
Chaucer 136
Chrysostomus, John 18,
    134, 146
Cicero 11, 23, 99
Colet, John 5, 6, 68, 71,
    74, 111, 119, 120, 130
Collegium Trilingue 8, 111

Dalburt, Johann of 110
Dickens, A. G. 86
Dimont, Max I. 152
Dionysius 116

Eckert, W. P. 48
Emerton, Ephvaim 130,
    141
Erikson, Eric 30, 137

Fisher, John St. 68, 71,
    74, 120, 130
Foxe, Richard 6

Francis I 111
Frederick III 18
Frederick the Wise 123
Freud, Sigmund 28, 132, 134, 146
Friedenthal, R. 15
Froben(ius), Johannes 8, 10
Fromm, Erich 150, 152

Gemmingen, Uriel von 58, 62, 64
Gillis, Peter 115
Glareanus, H. 8
Gregory VII, Pope 98, 122

Hacohen, Joseph 115
Harnack, Adolph 102
Haym, R. 22
Hegel, F. 163
Heitmueller, Wm. 154
Henry VIII 6
Hitler, Adolf 138, 139, 149
Hochstraten (Hoogstraten), Jacob 37, 55, 63, 71, 72, 74
Huizinga, Johan 102
Hutten, Ulrich von 64, 77, 130, 137

Ignatius of Loyola 6, 145
Innocent VIII, Pope 118
Inquisition 72, 84
Iqbal, Mohammed 159

Jackson, W. T. H. 131
Jacob, ben Yehiel Loens 18, 59
Jahoda, Marie 140, 143
James IV of Scotland 6

Jerome, St. 63, 146
Josel, Rabbi of Rossheim
   112
Julius II, Pope 46, 48, 140

Karben, Victor von 55, 58
Katzian, von 50
Kisch, Guido 15, 74, 81,
   82
Koerber, E. von 15, 41,
   100
Kluge, Otto 115
Kunigunde, sister of Emperor Maximilian 56

Langer, Wm. C. 138
Lascaris, John 6
Lates, Bonet de 64
Lazare, B. 96
Leo X, Pope 8, 64, 140
Lessing, Gotth. Ephraim
   50
Lifton, R. J. 30
Lipman, Rabbi Yom Tov
   51
Lister, Gerhard 69
Locher, G. W. 161
Loewenberg, Peter 143,
   144, 149, 150
Louvain, University of 5
Lullus, Raymond 50, 117
   118
Luther, Martin 8, 10, 20,
   21, 22, 38, 40, 46, 48,
   51, 74, 76, 77, 81, 82,
   87, 90, 100, 102, 116,
   119, 123, 133, 144

Mangan, J. J. 131, 132
Manutius, Aldus 6, 46,
   141
Margolin, Jean Claude 15

Maritain, M. J. 90, 137, 162
Masaryk, Thomas G. 161
Maximilian, Emperor 58, 60, 63, 82
Mazzeo, J. A. 158
Medigo, Del 119
Melanchthon, Philip 86, 97, 116
Montagu, College of 4
More, Sir Thomas 5, 6, 14, 68, 130
Moses de Leon 122
Mountjoy, Lord 5, 6
Mowrer, O. Hobert 105
Muenster, Sebastian 64
Musurus, Marcus 6

Nesen, W. 8
Neuenaar, Herman von 70
Nicolas of Lyra 18, 62, 63
Nichols, F. M. 116
Negri, Peter (Schwarz) 58, 62

Oecolompadius, J. 8, 78, 112
Ortuinus, Gratius 55, 56
Osborn, O. 158

Paul, St. 99, 145, 146
Pellican, K. 58, 109, 115
Pfefferkorn 18, 48, 50, 55, 56, 58, 60, 62, 68, 69, 70, 71, 74, 76
Pfeiffer, Rudolf 22
Phillips, M. M. 158
Philo of Alexandria 117
Pico della Mirandola 18, 58, 59, 62, 96, 97, 118, 119, 139, 158

Pirckheimer, Willibald 48, 68, 74
Pirenne, Henri 98
Poliakov, Leon 137
Popkin, Richard H. 11
Postell, Guillaume 97, 122, 123

Rand, Edward K. 14
Rashi, Rabbi Shelomoh ben Yishaq 18, 62
Reedijk, Cornelis 51
Renaudet, Augustine 102
Rengstorf, K. H. 50
Reuchlin, John 14, 18, 20, 37, 50, 58, 59, 60, 62, 63, 64, 66, 68, 69, 71, 72, 74, 76, 77, 78, 90, 95, 96, 97, 110, 111, 115, 116, 117, 119, 120, 122, 133, 139
Ricius, Paulus 82
Rokeach, Milton 144
Rubianus, Crotus 64
Rupp, Gordon E. 128

Savonarola, 119, 162
Schenk, V. W. D. 127, 128
Schlechta, Johannes 36
Seneca 8
Servetus, Michel 10, 98, 141
Sforno, Obadja of Cesena 18, 59
Skinner, B. F. 160
Smith, John 141
Socrates 105
Spinoza, Barukh Benedict 91

Spitz, Lewis 31, 38
Standonck, Jan 4
Stern, Selma 112
Stuart, Alexander 6
Stunica, Jacob Lopez 48, 139

Taylor, H. O. 51
Thomas, St. of Aquinas 96
Thompson, Craig R. 97, 99
Thornton, A. P. 27
Tongern, Arnold of 55
Trieste, Isaac 60

Urban V, Pope 118

Valla, Lorenzo 5
Valladolid, University of 110
Vellarius, Johannes 112
Viterbo, Egidio de 64
Vives 114
Volz, Paul 87

Warham, Wm. 6
Weber, Max 145
Weinstock, Heinrich 159
Welzig, Werner 42, 142
Werthemann, A. 127
White Jr., Lynn 22
Widmannstadt 64
Wilhelm II, Kaiser 149
Winckler, Gerhard B. 3, 17
Wolman, Benjamin B. 30, 86, 114, 131
Woolsey, Thomas 74, 76
Woodward, W. H. 97, 102

Zion, Jonathan Levi 60
Zweig, St. 15
Zwingli, Ulrich von 77,
    78, 109